Walt Whitman, Richard Maurice Bucke

The Wound Dresser

A Series of Letters Written From the Hospitals in Washington During...

Walt Whitman, Richard Maurice Bucke

The Wound Dresser

A Series of Letters Written From the Hospitals in Washington During...

ISBN/EAN: 9783337015336

Printed in Europe, USA, Canada, Australia, Japan

Cover: Foto ©ninafisch / pixelio.de

More available books at **www.hansebooks.com**

THE
WOUND DRESSER

A Series of Letters
Written from the Hospitals in Washington
During the War of the Rebellion

By
WALT WHITMAN

Edited by
RICHARD MAURICE BUCKE, M.D.
One of Whitman's Literary Executors

Boston
SMALL, MAYNARD & COMPANY
1898

*But in silence, in dreams' projections,
While the world of gain and appearance and mirth goes on,
So soon what is over forgotten, and waves wash the imprints
    off the sand,
With hinged knees returning I enter the doors, (while for you
    up there,
Whoever you are, follow without noise and be of strong
    heart.)*

*I onward go, I stop,
With hinged knees and steady hand to dress wounds,
I am firm with each, the pangs are sharp yet unavoidable,
One turns to me his appealing eyes — poor boy! I never
    knew you,
Yet I think I could not refuse this moment to die for you, if
    that would save you.*

*I am faithful, I do not give out,
The fractur'd thigh, the knee, the wound in the abdomen,
These and more I dress with impassive hand, (yet deep in my
    breast a fire, a burning flame.)*

*Thus in silence, in dreams' projections,
Returning, resuming, I thread my way through the hospitals,
The hurt and wounded I pacify with soothing hand,
I sit by the restless all the dark night, some are so young,
Some suffer so much, I recall the experience sweet and sad,
(Many a soldier's loving arms about this neck have cross'd
    and rested,
Many a soldier's kiss dwells on these bearded lips.)*

The Wound Dresser.

PREFACE

AS introduction to these letters from Walt Whitman to his mother, I have availed myself of three of Whitman's communications to the press covering the time during which the material which composes this volume was being written. These communications (parts of which, but in no case the whole, were used by Whitman in his "Memoranda of the Secession War") seem to me to form, in spite of certain duplications, which to my mind have the force, not the weakness, of repetition, quite an ideal background to the letters to Mrs. Whitman, since they give a full and free description of the circumstances and surroundings in the midst of which those were composed. Readers who desire a still more extended account of the man himself, his work and environment at that time, may consult with profit the Editor's "Walt Whitman" (pp. 34–44), O'Connor's "Good Gray Poet" (included in that volume, pp. 99–130), "Specimen Days" (pp. 26–63, included in Walt Whitman's "Complete Prose Works"), and above all the section of "Leaves of Grass" called "Drum-Taps." I do not believe that it is in the power of any man now living to make an important addition to the vivid picture of those days and nights in the hospitals drawn by Whitman himself and to be found in his published prose and verse, and, above all, in the living words of the present letters to his mother. These

Preface

last were written on the spot, as the scenes and incidents, in all their living and sombre colors, passed before his eyes, while his mind and heart were full of the sights and sounds, the episodes and agonies, of those terrible hours. How could any one writing in cold blood, to-day, hope to add words of any value to those he wrote then?

Perhaps, in conclusion, it may be as well to repeat what was said in the introduction to a former volume, — that these letters make no pretensions as literature. They are, as indeed is all that Whitman has written (as he himself has over and over again said), something quite different from that — something much less to the average cultured and learned man, something much more to the man or woman who comes within range of their attraction. But doubtless the critics will still insist that, if they are not literature, they ought to be, or otherwise should not be printed, failing (as is their wont) to comprehend that there are other qualities and characteristics than the literary, some of them as important and as valuable, which may be more or less adequately conveyed by print.

R. M. B.

CONTENTS

	Page
THE GREAT ARMY OF THE WOUNDED	1
LIFE AMONG FIFTY THOUSAND SOLDIERS	11
HOSPITAL VISITS	21
LETTERS OF 1862–3	47
LETTERS OF 1864	143

THE GREAT ARMY OF THE WOUNDED

THE military hospitals, convalescent camps, etc., in Washington and its neighborhood, sometimes contain over fifty thousand sick and wounded men. Every form of wound (the mere sight of some of them having been known to make a tolerably hardy visitor faint away), every kind of malady, like a long procession, with typhoid fever and diarrhœa at the head as leaders, are here in steady motion. The soldier's hospital! how many sleepless nights, how many women's tears, how many long and waking hours and days of suspense, from every one of the Middle, Eastern, and Western States, have concentrated here! Our own New York, in the form of hundreds and thousands of her young men, may consider herself here — Pennsylvania, Ohio, Indiana, and all the West and Northwest the same — and all the New England States the same.

Upon a few of these hospitals I have been almost daily calling as a missionary, on my own account, for the sustenance and consolation of some of the most needy cases of sick and dying men, for the last two months. One has much to learn to do good in these places. Great tact is required. These are not like other hospitals. By far the greatest proportion (I should say five sixths) of the patients are American young men, intelligent, of independent spirit, tender feelings, used

The Wound Dresser

to a hardy and healthy life; largely the farmers are represented by their sons — largely the mechanics and workingmen of the cities. Then they are soldiers. All these points must be borne in mind.

People through our Northern cities have little or no idea of the great and prominent feature which these military hospitals and convalescent camps make in and around Washington. There are not merely two or three or a dozen, but some fifty of them, of different degrees of capacity. Some have a thousand and more patients. The newspapers here find it necessary to print every day a directory of the hospitals — a long list, something like what a directory of the churches would be in New York, Philadelphia, or Boston.

The Government (which really tries, I think, to do the best and quickest it can for these sad necessities) is gradually settling down to adopt the plan of placing the hospitals in clusters of one-story wooden barracks, with their accompanying tents and sheds for cooking and all needed purposes. Taking all things into consideration, no doubt these are best adapted to the purpose; better than using churches and large public buildings like the Patent office. These sheds now adopted are long, one-story edifices, sometimes ranged along in a row, with their heads to the street, and numbered either alphabetically, Wards A or B, C, D, and so on; or Wards 1, 2, 3, etc. The middle one will be marked by a flagstaff, and is the office of the establishment, with rooms for

The Great Army of the Wounded

the ward surgeons, etc. One of these sheds, or wards, will contain sixty cots; sometimes, on an emergency, they move them close together, and crowd in more. Some of the barracks are larger, with, of course, more inmates. Frequently there are tents, more comfortable here than one might think, whatever they may be down in the army.

Each ward has a ward-master, and generally a nurse for every ten or twelve men. A ward surgeon has, generally, two wards — although this varies. Some of the wards have a woman nurse; the Armory-square wards have some very good ones. The one in Ward E is one of the best.

A few weeks ago the vast area of the second story of that noblest of Washington buildings, the Patent office, was crowded close with rows of sick, badly wounded, and dying soldiers. They were placed in three very large apartments. I went there several times. It was a strange, solemn, and, with all its features of suffering and death, a sort of fascinating sight. I went sometimes at night to soothe and relieve particular cases ; some, I found, needed a little cheering up and friendly consolation at that time, for they went to sleep better afterwards. Two of the immense apartments are filled with high and ponderous glass cases crowded with models in miniature of every kind of utensil, machine, or invention it ever entered into the mind of man to conceive, and with curiosities and foreign presents. Between these cases were lateral openings, perhaps eight

The Wound Dresser

feet wide, and quite deep, and in these were placed many of the sick; besides a great long double row of them up and down through the middle of the hall. Many of them were very bad cases, wounds and amputations. Then there was a gallery running above the hall, in which there were beds also. It was, indeed, a curious scene at night when lit up. The glass cases, the beds, the sick, the gallery above and the marble pavement under foot; the suffering, and the fortitude to bear it in the various degrees; occasionally, from some, the groan that could not be repressed; sometimes a poor fellow dying, with emaciated face and glassy eyes, the nurse by his side, the doctor also there, but no friend, no relative — such were the sights but lately in the Patent office. The wounded have since been removed from there, and it is now vacant again.

Of course there are among these thousands of prostrated soldiers in hospital here all sorts of individual cases. On recurring to my note-book, I am puzzled which cases to select to illustrate the average of these young men and their experiences. I may here say, too, in general terms, that I could not wish for more candor and manliness, among all their sufferings, than I find among them.

Take this case in Ward 6, Campbell hospital: a young man from Plymouth county, Massachusetts; a farmer's son, aged about twenty or twenty-one; a soldierly, American young fellow, but with sensitive and tender feelings. Most of De-

The Great Army of the Wounded

cember and January last he lay very low, and for quite a while I never expected he would recover. He had become prostrated with an obstinate diarrhœa: his stomach would hardly keep the least thing down; he was vomiting half the time. But that was hardly the worst of it. Let me tell his story — it is but one of thousands.

He had been some time sick with his regiment in the field, in front, but did his duty as long as he could; was in the battle of Fredericksburg; soon after was put in the regimental hospital. He kept getting worse — could not eat anything they had there; the doctor told him nothing could be done for him there. The poor fellow had fever also; received (perhaps it could not be helped) little or no attention; lay on the ground, getting worse. Toward the latter part of December, very much enfeebled, he was sent up from the front, from Falmouth station, in an open platform car (such as hogs are transported upon North), and dumped with a crowd of others on the boat at Aquia creek, falling down like a rag where they deposited him, too weak and sick to sit up or help himself at all. No one spoke to him or assisted him; he had nothing to eat or drink; was used (amid the great crowds of sick) either with perfect indifference, or, as in two or three instances, with heartless brutality.

On the boat, when night came and when the air grew chilly, he tried a long time to undo the blankets he had in his knapsack, but was too feeble. He asked one of the employees, who was moving

The Wound Dresser

around deck, for a moment's assistance to get the blankets. The man asked him back if he could not get them himself. He answered, no, he had been trying for more than half an hour, and found himself too weak. The man rejoined, he might then go without them, and walked off. So H. lay chilled and damp on deck all night, without anything under or over him, while two good blankets were within reach. It caused him a great injury — nearly cost him his life.

Arrived at Washington, he was brought ashore and again left on the wharf, or above it, amid the great crowds, as before, without any nourishment — not a drink for his parched mouth; no kind hand had offered to cover his face from the forenoon sun. Conveyed at last some two miles by the ambulance to the hospital, and assigned a bed (Bed 49, Ward 6, Campbell hospital, January and February, 1863), he fell down exhausted upon the bed. But the ward-master (he has since been changed) came to him with a growling order to get up: the rules, he said, permitted no man to lie down in that way with his own clothes on; he must sit up — must first go to the bath-room, be washed, and have his clothes completely changed. (A very good rule, properly applied.) He was taken to the bath-room and scrubbed well with cold water. The attendants, callous for a while, were soon alarmed, for suddenly the half-frozen and lifeless body fell limpsy in their hands, and they hurried it back to the cot, plainly insensible, perhaps dying.

The Great Army of the Wounded

Poor boy! the long train of exhaustion, deprivation, rudeness, no food, no friendly word or deed, but all kinds of upstart airs and impudent, unfeeling speeches and deeds, from all kinds of small officials (and some big ones), cutting like razors into that sensitive heart, had at last done the job. He now lay, at times out of his head but quite silent, asking nothing of any one, for some days, with death getting a closer and a surer grip upon him; he cared not, or rather he welcomed death. His heart was broken. He felt the struggle to keep up any longer to be useless. God, the world, humanity — all had abandoned him. It would feel so good to shut his eyes forever on the cruel things around him and toward him.

As luck would have it, at this time I found him. I was passing down Ward No. 6 one day about dusk (4th January, I think), and noticed his glassy eyes, with a look of despair and hopelessness, sunk low in his thin, pallid-brown young face. One learns to divine quickly in the hospital, and as I stopped by him and spoke some commonplace remark (to which he made no reply), I saw as I looked that it was a case for ministering to the affection first, and other nourishment and medicines afterward. I sat down by him without any fuss; talked a little; soon saw that it did him good; led him to talk a little himself; got him somewhat interested; wrote a letter for him to his folks in Massachusetts (to L. H. Campbell, Plymouth county); soothed him down as I saw

The Wound Dresser

he was getting a little too much agitated, and tears in his eyes; gave him some small gifts, and told him I should come again soon. (He has told me since that this little visit, at that hour, just saved him; a day more, and it would have been perhaps too late.)

Of course I did not forget him, for he was a young fellow to interest any one. He remained very sick — vomiting much every day, frequent diarrhœa, and also something like bronchitis, the doctor said. For a while I visited him almost every day, cheered him up, took him some little gifts, and gave him small sums of money (he relished a drink of new milk, when it was brought through the ward for sale). For a couple of weeks his condition was uncertain — sometimes I thought there was no chance for him at all; but of late he is doing better — is up and dressed, and goes around more and more (February 21) every day. He will not die, but will recover.

The other evening, passing through the ward, he called me — he wanted to say a few words, particular. I sat down by his side on the cot in the dimness of the long ward, with the wounded soldiers there in their beds, ranging up and down. H. told me I had saved his life. He was in the deepest earnest about it. It was one of those things that repay a soldiers' hospital missionary a thousandfold — one of the hours he never forgets.

A benevolent person, with the right qualities and tact, cannot, perhaps, make a better investment of himself, at present, anywhere upon the

The Great Army of the Wounded

varied surface of the whole of this big world, than in these military hospitals, among such thousands of most interesting young men. The army is very young — and so much more American than I supposed. Reader, how can I describe to you the mute appealing look that rolls and moves from many a manly eye, from many a sick cot, following you as you walk slowly down one of these wards? To see these, and to be incapable of responding to them, except in a few cases (so very few compared to the whole of the suffering men), is enough to make one's heart crack. I go through in some cases, cheering up the men, distributing now and then little sums of money — and, regularly, letter-paper and envelopes, oranges, tobacco, jellies, etc., etc.

Many things invite comment, and some of them sharp criticism, in these hospitals. The Government, as I said, is anxious and liberal in its practice toward its sick; but the work has to be left, in its personal application to the men, to hundreds of officials of one grade or another about the hospitals, who are sometimes entirely lacking in the right qualities. There are tyrants and shysters in all positions, and especially those dressed in subordinate authority. Some of the ward doctors are careless, rude, capricious, needlessly strict. One I found who prohibited the men from all enlivening amusements; I found him sending men to the guard-house for the most trifling offence. In general, perhaps, the officials — especially the new ones, with their straps or

The Wound Dresser

badges — put on too many airs. Of all places in the world, the hospitals of American young men and soldiers, wounded in the volunteer service of their country, ought to be exempt from mere conventional military airs and etiquette of shoulder-straps. But they are not exempt.

W. W.

From the New York Times, February 26, 1863.

LIFE AMONG FIFTY THOUSAND SOLDIERS

OUR Brooklyn people, not only from having so many hundreds of their own kith and kin, and almost everybody some friend or acquaintance, here in the clustering military hospitals of Washington, would doubtless be glad to get some account of these establishments, but also to satisfy that compound of benevolence and generosity which marks Brooklyn, I have sometimes thought, more than any other city in the world. A military hospital here in Washington is a little city by itself, and contains a larger population than most of the well-known country towns down in the Queens and Suffolk county portions of Long Island. I say one of the Government hospitals here is a little city in itself, and there are some fifty of these hospitals in the District of Columbia alone. In them are collected the tens of thousands of sick and wounded soldiers, the legacies of many a bloody battle and of the exposure of two years of camp life. I find these places full of significance. They have taken up my principal time and labor for some months past. Imagine a long, one-story wooden shed, like a short, wide ropewalk, well whitewashed; then cluster ten or a dozen of these together, with several smaller sheds and tents, and you have the soldiers' hospital as generally adopted here. It will contain perhaps six or seven hundred men, or perhaps a

The Wound Dresser

thousand, and occasionally more still. There is a regular staff and a sub-staff of big and little officials. Military etiquette is observed, and it is getting to become very stiff. I shall take occasion, before long, to show up some of this ill-fitting nonsense. The harvest is large, the gleaners few. Beginning at first with casual visits to these establishments to see some of the Brooklyn men, wounded or sick, here, I became by degrees more and more drawn in, until I have now been for many weeks quite a devotee to the business — a regular self-appointed missionary to these thousands and tens of thousands of wounded and sick young men here, left upon Government hands, many of them languishing, many of them dying. I am not connected with any society, but go on my own individual account, and to the work that appears to be called for. Almost every day, and frequently in the evenings, I visit, in this informal way, one after another of the wards of a hospital, and always find cases enough where I can be of service. Cases enough, do I say? Alas! there is, perhaps, not one ward or tent, out of the seven or eight hundred now hereabout filled with sick, in which I am sure I might not profitably devote every hour of my life to the abstract work of consolation and sustenance for its suffering inmates. And indeed, beyond that, a person feels that in some one of these crowded wards he would like to pick out two or three cases and devote himself wholly to them. Meanwhile, however, to do the best that is permitted, I go around, distributing myself and

Life among Fifty Thousand Soldiers

the contents of my pockets and haversack in infinitesimal quantities, with faith that nearly all of it will, somehow or other, fall on good ground. In many cases, where I find a soldier "dead broke" and pretty sick, I give half a tumbler of good jelly. I carry a good-sized jar to a ward, have it opened, get a spoon, and taking the head nurse in tow, I go around and distribute it to the most appropriate cases. To others I give an orange or an apple; to others some spiced fruits; to others a small quantity of pickles. Many want tobacco: I do not encourage any of the boys in its use, but where I find they crave it I supply them. I always carry some, cut up in small plugs, in my pocket. Then I have commissions: some New York or Connecticut, or other soldier, will be going home on sick leave, or perhaps discharged, and I must fit him out with good new undershirt, drawers, stockings, etc.

But perhaps the greatest welcome is for writing paper, envelopes, etc. I find these always a rare reliance. When I go into a new ward, I always carry two or three quires of paper and a good lot of envelopes, and walk up and down and circulate them around to those who desire them. Then some will want pens, pencils, etc. In some hospitals there is quite a plenty of reading matter; but others, where it is needed, I supply.

By these and like means one comes to be better acquainted with individual cases, and so learns every day peculiar and interesting character, and gets on intimate and soon affectionate terms with

The Wound Dresser

noble American young men; and now is where the real good begins to be done, after all. Here, I will egotistically confess, I like to flourish. Even in a medical point of view it is one of the greatest things; and in a surgical point of view, the same. I can testify that friendship has literally cured a fever, and the medicine of daily affection, a bad wound. In these sayings are the final secret of carrying out well the rôle of a hospital missionary for our soldiers, which I tell for those who will understand them.

As I write, I have lying before me a little discarded note-book, filled with memoranda of things wanted by the sick — special cases. I use up one of these little books in a week. See from this sample, for instance, after walking through a ward or two: Bed 53 wants some liquorice; Bed 6 — erysipelas — bring some raspberry vinegar to make a cooling drink, with water; Bed 18 wants a good book — a romance; Bed 25 — a manly, friendly young fellow, H. D. B., of the Twenty-seventh Connecticut, an independent young soul — refuses money and eatables, so I will bring him a pipe and tobacco, for I see he much enjoys a smoke; Bed 45 — sore throat and cough — wants horehound candy; Bed 11, when I come again, don't forget to write a letter for him; etc. The wants are a long and varied list: some need to be humored and forgotten, others need to be especially remembered and obeyed. One poor German, dying — in the last stage of consumption — wished me to find him, in Washington, a German Lutheran clergyman,

Life among Fifty Thousand Soldiers

and send him to him; I did so. One patient will want nothing but a toothpick, another a comb, and so on. All whims are represented, and all the States. There are many New York State soldiers here; also Pennsylvanians. I find, of course, many from Massachusetts, Connecticut, and all the New England States, and from the Western and Northwestern States. Five sixths of the soldiers are young men.

Among other cases of young men from our own city of Brooklyn I have encountered and have had much to do with in hospital here, is John Lowery, wounded, and arm amputated, at Fredericksburg. I saw this young fellow down there last December, immediately after the battle, lying on a blanket on the ground, the stump of his arm bandaged, but he not a bit disheartened. He was soon afterward sent up from the front by way of Aquia creek, and has for the past three months been in the Campbell hospital here, in Ward 6, on the gain slowly but steadily. He thinks a great deal of his physician here, Dr. Frank Hinkle, and as some fifty other soldiers in the ward do the same, and bear testimony in their hearty gratitude, and medical and surgical imprisonment, to the quality of Dr. H., I think he deserves honorable mention in this letter to the people of our city — especially as another Brooklyn soldier in Ward 6, Amos H. Vliet, expresses the same feeling of obligation to the doctor for his faithfulness and kindness. Vliet and Lowery both belong to that old war regiment

The Wound Dresser

whose flag has flaunted through more than a score of hot-contested battles, the Fifty-first New York, Colonel Potter; and it is to be remembered that no small portion of the fame of this old veteran regiment may be claimed near home, for many of her officers and men are from Brooklyn. The friends of these two young soldiers will have a chance to talk to them soon in Brooklyn. I have seen a good deal of Jack Lowery, and I find him, and heard of him on the field, as a brave, soldierly fellow. Amos Vliet, too, made a first-rate soldier. He has had frozen feet pretty bad, but now better. Occasionally I meet some of the Brooklyn Fourteenth. In Ward E of Armory hospital I found a member of Company C of that regiment, Isaac Snyder; he is now acting as nurse there, and makes a very good one. Charles Dean, of Co. H of the same regiment, is in Ward A of Armory, acting as ward-master. I also got very well acquainted with a young man of the Brooklyn Fourteenth who lay sick some time in Ward F; he has lately got his discharge and gone home. I have met with others in the H-street and Patent-office hospitals. Colonel Fowler, of the Fourteenth, is in charge, I believe, of the convalescent camp at Alexandria. Lieutenant-Colonel Debevoise is in Brooklyn, in poor health, I am sorry to say. Thus the Brooklyn invalids are scattered around.

Off in the mud, a mile east of the Capitol, I found the other day, in Emory hospital there, in Ward C, three Brooklyn soldiers — Allen V.

Life among Fifty Thousand Soldiers

King, Michael Lally, and Patrick Hennessy; none of them, however, are very sick.

At a rough guess, I should say I have met from one hundred and fifty to two hundred young and middle-aged men whom I specifically found to be Brooklyn persons. Many of them I recognized as having seen their faces before, and very many of them knew me. Some said they had known me from boyhood. Some would call to me as I passed down a ward, and tell me they had seen me in Brooklyn. I have had this happen at night, and have been entreated to stop and sit down and take the hand of a sick and restless boy, and talk to him and comfort him awhile, for old Brooklyn's sake.

Some pompous and every way improper persons, of course, get in power in hospitals, and have full swing over the helpless soldiers. There is great state kept at Judiciary-square hospital, for instance. An individual who probably has been waiter somewhere for years past has got into the high and mighty position of sergeant-of-arms at this hospital; he is called "Red Stripe" (from his artillery trimmings) by the patients, of whom he is at the same time the tyrant and the laughing-stock. Going in to call on some sick New York soldiers here the other afternoon, I was stopped and treated to a specimen of the airs of this powerful officer. Surely the Government would do better to send such able-bodied loafers down into service in front, where they could earn their rations, than keep them here in the idle and

The Wound Dresser

shallow sinecures of military guard over a collection of sick soldiers to give insolence to their visitors and friends. I found a shallow old person also here named Dr. Hall, who told me he had been eighteen years in the service. I must give this Judiciary establishment the credit, from my visits to it, of saying that while in all the other hospitals I met with general cordiality and deference among the doctors, ward officers, nurses, etc., I have found more impudence and more dandy doctorism and more needless airs at this Judiciary, than in all the twoscore other establishments in and around Washington. But the corps of management at the Judiciary has a bad name anyhow, and I only specify it here to put on record the general opinion, and in hopes it may help in calling the attention of the Government to a remedy. For this hospital is half filled with New York soldiers, many noble fellows, and many sad and interesting cases. Of course there are exceptions of good officials here, and some of the women nurses are excellent, but the Empire State has no reason to be over-satisfied with this hospital.

But I should say, in conclusion, that the earnest and continued desire of the Government, and much devoted labor, are given to make the military hospitals here as good as they can be, considering all things. I find no expense spared, and great anxiety manifested in the highest quarters, to do well by the national sick. I meet with first-class surgeons in charge of many of the

Life among Fifty Thousand Soldiers

hospitals, and often the ward surgeons, medical cadets, and head nurses, are fully faithful and competent. Dr. Bliss, head of Armory-square, and Dr. Baxter, head of Campbell, seem to me to try to do their best, and to be excellent in their posts. Dr. Bowen, one of the ward surgeons of Armory, I have known to fight as hard for many a poor fellow's life under his charge as a lioness would fight for her young. I mention such cases because I think they deserve it, on public grounds.

I thought I would include in my letter a few cases of soldiers, especially interesting, out of my note-book, but I find that my story has already been spun out to sufficient length. I shall continue here in Washington for the present, and may-be for the summer, to work as a missionary, after my own style, among these hospitals, for I find it in some respects curiously fascinating, with all its sadness. Nor do I find it ended by my doing some good to the sick and dying soldiers. They do me good in return, more than I do them.

W. W.

From the Brooklyn Eagle, *March 19, 1863.*

HOSPITAL VISITS

AS this tremendous war goes on, the public interest becomes more general and gathers more and more closely about the wounded, the sick, and the Government hospitals, the surgeons, and all appertaining to the medical department of the army. Up to the date of this writing (December 9, 1864) there have been, as I estimate, near four hundred thousand cases under treatment, and there are to-day, probably, taking the whole service of the United States, two hundred thousand, or an approximation to that number, on the doctors' list. Half of these are comparatively slight ailments or hurts. Every family has directly or indirectly some representative among this vast army of the wounded and sick.

The following sketch is made to gratify the general interest in this field of the war, and also for a few special persons through whose means alone I have aided the men. It extends over a period of two years, coming down to the present hour, and exhibits the army hospitals at Washington, the camp hospitals in the field, etc. A very few cases are given as specimens of thousands. The account may be relied upon as faithful, though rapidly thrown together. It will put the reader in as direct contact as may be with scenes, sights, and cases of these immense hospitals. As will be seen, it begins back two years since, at a very gloomy period of the contest.

The Wound Dresser

Began my visits (December 21, 1862) among the camp hospitals in the Army of the Potomac, under General Burnside. Spent a good part of the day in a large brick mansion on the banks of the Rappahannock, immediately opposite Fredericksburg. It is used as a hospital since the battle, and seems to have received only the worst cases. Outdoors, at the foot of a tree, within ten yards of the front of the house, I notice a heap of amputated feet, legs, arms, hands, etc. — about a load for a one-horse cart. Several dead bodies lie near, each covered with its brown woollen blanket. In the dooryard, toward the river, are fresh graves, mostly of officers, their names on pieces of barrel staves or broken board, stuck in the dirt. (Most of these bodies were subsequently taken up and transported North to their friends.)

The house is quite crowded, everything impromptu, no system, all bad enough, but I have no doubt the best that can be done; all the wounds pretty bad, some frightful, the men in their old clothes, unclean and bloody. Some of the wounded are rebel officers, prisoners. One, a Mississippian — a captain — hit badly in the leg, I talked with some time; he asked me for papers, which I gave him. (I saw him three months afterward in Washington, with leg amputated, doing well.)

I went through the rooms, down stairs and up. Some of the men were dying. I had nothing to give at that visit, but wrote a few letters to

Hospital Visits

folks home, mothers, etc. Also talked to three or four who seemed most susceptible to it, and needing it.

December 22 to 31.—Am among the regimental brigade and division hospitals somewhat. Few at home realize that these are merely tents, and sometimes very poor ones, the wounded lying on the ground, lucky if their blanket is spread on a layer of pine or hemlock twigs, or some leaves. No cots; seldom even a mattress on the ground. It is pretty cold. I go around from one case to another. I do not see that I can do any good, but I cannot leave them. Once in a while some youngster holds on to me convulsively, and I do what I can for him; at any rate stop with him, and sit near him for hours, if he wishes it.

Besides the hospitals, I also go occasionally on long tours through the camps, talking with the men, etc.; sometimes at night among the groups around the fires, in their shebang enclosures of bushes. I soon get acquainted anywhere in camp with officers or men, and am always well used. Sometimes I go down on picket with the regiments I know best.

As to rations, the army here at present seems to be tolerably well supplied, and the men have enough, such as it is. Most of the regiments lodge in the flimsy little shelter tents. A few have built themselves huts of logs and mud, with fireplaces.

I might give a long list of special cases, inter-

The Wound Dresser

esting items of the wounded men here, but have not space.

Left Falmouth, January, 1863, by Aquia creek railroad, and so on Government steamer up the Potomac. Many wounded were with us on cars and boat. The cars were just common platform ones. The railroad journey of ten or twelve miles was made mostly before sunrise. The soldiers guarding the road came out from their tents or shebangs of bushes with rumpled hair and half-awake look. Those on duty were walking their posts, some on banks over us, others down far below the level of the track. I saw large cavalry camps off the road. At Aquia Creek Landing were numbers of wounded going North. While I waited some three hours, I went around among them. Several wanted word sent home to parents, brothers, wives, etc., which I did for them (by mail the next day from Washington). On the boat I had my hands full. One poor fellow died going up.

Am now (January, February, etc., 1863) in and around Washington, daily visiting the hospitals. Am much in Campbell, Patent-office, Eighth-street, H-street, Armory-square, and others. Am now able to do a little good, having money (as almoner of others home), and getting experience. I would like to give lists of cases, for there is no end to the interesting ones; but it is impossible without making a large volume, or rather several volumes. I must, therefore, let one or two days' visits at this time suffice

Hospital Visits

as specimens of scores and hundreds of subsequent ones, through the ensuing spring, summer, and fall, and, indeed, down to the present week.

Sunday, January 25.— Afternoon and till 9 in the evening, visited Campbell hospital. Attended specially to one case in Ward I, very sick with pleurisy and typhoid fever, young man, farmer's son — D. F. Russell, Company E, Sixtieth New York — down-hearted and feeble; a long time before he would take any interest; soothed and cheered him gently; wrote a letter home to his mother, in Malone, Franklin county, N. Y., at his request; gave him some fruit and one or two other gifts; enveloped and directed his letter, etc. Then went thoroughly through Ward 6; observed every case in the ward (without, I think, missing one); found some cases I thought needed little sums of money; supplied them (sums of perhaps thirty, twenty-five, twenty, or fifteen cents); distributed a pretty bountiful supply of cheerful reading matter, and gave perhaps some twenty to thirty persons, each one some little gift, such as oranges, apples, sweet crackers, figs, etc., etc., etc.

Thursday, January 29.— Devoted the main part of the day, from 11 to 3.30 o'clock, to Armory-square hospital; went pretty thoroughly through Wards F, G, H, and I — some fifty cases in each ward. In Ward H supplied the men throughout with writing paper and a stamped envelope each, also some cheerful reading matter; distributed in small portions, about half of it in this ward, to proper subjects, a

The Wound Dresser

large jar of first-rate preserved berries; also other small gifts. In Wards G, H, and I, found several cases I thought good subjects for small sums of money, which I furnished in each case. The poor wounded men often come up "dead broke," and it helps their spirits to have even the small sum I give them. My paper and envelopes all gone, but distributed a good lot of amusing reading matter; also, as I thought judicious, tobacco, oranges, apples, etc. Some very interesting cases in Ward I: Charles Miller, Bed No. 19, Company D, Fifty-third Pennsylvania, is only sixteen years of age, very bright, courageous boy, left leg amputated below the knee; next bed below him, young lad very sick — gave the two each appropriate gifts; in the bed above also amputation of the left leg — gave him a part of a jar of raspberries; Bed No. 1, this ward, gave a small sum also; also to a soldier on crutches, sitting on his bed near.

Evening, same day. — Went to see D. F. R., Campbell hospital, before alluded to; found him remarkably changed for the better — up and dressed (quite a triumph; he afterwards got well and went back to his regiment). Distributed in the wards a quantity of note-paper and forty or fifty, mostly paid, envelopes, of which the men were much in need; also a four-pound bag of gingersnaps I bought at a baker's in Seventh street.

Here is a case of a soldier I found among the crowded cots in the Patent hospital — (they have removed most of the men of late and broken up

Hospital Visits

that hospital). He likes to have some one to talk to, and we will listen to him. He got badly wounded in the leg and side at Fredericksburg that eventful Saturday, 13th December. He lay the succeeding two days and nights helpless on the field, between the city and those grim batteries, for his company and his regiment had been compelled to leave him to his fate. To make matters worse, he lay with his head slightly down hill, and could not help himself. At the end of some fifty hours he was brought off, with other wounded, under a flag of truce.

We ask him how the Rebels treated him during those two days and nights within reach of them — whether they came to him — whether they abused him? He answers that several of the Rebels, soldiers and others, came to him, at one time and another. A couple of them, who were together, spoke roughly and sarcastically, but did no act. One middle-aged man, however, who seemed to be moving around the field among the dead and wounded for benevolent purposes, came to him in a way he will never forget. This man treated our soldier kindly, bound up his wounds, cheered him, gave him a couple of biscuits gave him a drink of whiskey and water, asked him if he could eat some beef. This good Secesh, however, did not change our soldier's position, for it might have caused the blood to burst from the wounds where they were clotted and stagnated. Our soldier is from Pennsylvania; has had a pretty severe time; the wounds proved to be bad

The Wound Dresser

ones. But he retains a good heart, and is at present on the gain.

It is not uncommon for the men to remain on the field this way, one, two, or even four or five days.

I continue among the hospitals during March, April, etc., without intermission. My custom is to go through a ward, or a collection of wards, endeavoring to give some trifle to each, without missing any. Even a sweet biscuit, a sheet of paper, or a passing word of friendliness, or but a look or nod, if no more. In this way I go through large numbers without delaying, yet do not hurry. I find out the general mood of the ward at the time; sometimes see that there is a heavy weight of listlessness prevailing, and the whole ward wants cheering up. I perhaps read to the men, to break the spell, calling them around me, careful to sit away from the cot of any one who is very bad with sickness or wounds. Also I find out, by going through in this way, the cases that need special attention, and can then devote proper time to them. Of course I am very cautious, among the patients, in giving them food. I always confer with the doctor, or find out from the nurse or ward-master about a new case. But I soon get sufficiently familiar with what is to be avoided, and learn also to judge almost intuitively what is best.

I do a good deal of writing letters by the bedside, of course — writing all kinds, including love letters. Many sick and wounded soldiers have

Hospital Visits

not written home to parents, brothers, sisters, and even wives, for one reason or another, for a long, long time. Some are poor writers; some cannot get paper and envelopes; many have an aversion to writing, because they dread to worry the folks at home — the facts about them are so sad to tell. I always encourage the men to write, and promptly write for them.

As I write this, in May, 1863, the wounded have begun to arrive from Hooker's command, from bloody Chancellorsville. I was down among the first arrivals. The men in charge of them told me the bad cases were yet to come. If that is so, I pity them, for these are bad enough. You ought to see the scene of the wounded arriving at the landing here, foot of Sixth street, at night. Two boat-loads came about half-past seven last night. A little after eight it rained, a long and violent shower. The poor, pale, helpless soldiers had been debarked, and lay around on the wharf and neighborhood, anywhere. The rain was, probably, grateful to them; at any rate they were exposed to it.

The few torches light up the spectacle. All around on the wharf, on the ground, out on side places, etc., the men are lying on blankets, old quilts, etc., with the bloody rags bound around their heads, arms, legs, etc. The attendants are few, and at night few outsiders also — only a few hard-worked transportation men and drivers. (The wounded are getting to be common, and people grow callous.) The men, whatever their

The Wound Dresser

condition, lie there and patiently wait till their turn comes to be taken up. Near by the ambulances are now arriving in clusters, and one after another is called to back up and take its load. Extreme cases are sent off on stretchers. The men generally make little or no ado, whatever their sufferings — a few groans that cannot be repressed, and occasionally a scream of pain as they lift a man into the ambulance.

To-day, as I write, hundreds more are expected; and to-morrow and the next day more, and so on for many days.

The soldiers are nearly all young men, and far more Americans than is generally supposed — I should say nine tenths are native born. Among the arrivals from Chancellorsville I find a large proportion of Ohio, Indiana, and Illinois men. As usual there are all sorts of wounds. Some of the men are fearfully burnt from the explosion of artillery caissons. One ward has a long row of officers, some with ugly hurts. Yesterday was perhaps worse than usual: amputations are going on; the attendants are dressing wounds. As you pass by you must be on your guard where you look. I saw, the other day, a gentleman, a visitor, apparently from curiosity, in one of the wards, stop and turn a moment to look at an awful wound they were probing, etc.; he turned pale, and in a moment more he had fainted away and fallen on the floor.

I buy, during the hot weather, boxes of oranges from time to time, and distribute them

Hospital Visits

among the men; also preserved peaches and other fruits; also lemons and sugar for lemonade. Tobacco is also much in demand. Large numbers of the men come up, as usual, without a cent of money. Through the assistance of friends in Brooklyn and Boston, I am again able to help many of those that fall in my way. It is only a small sum in each case, but it is much to them. As before, I go around daily and talk with the men, to cheer them up.

My note-books are full of memoranda of the cases of this summer, and the wounded from Chancellorsville, but space forbids my transcribing them.

As I sit writing this paragraph (sundown, Thursday, June 25) I see a train of about thirty huge four-horse wagons, used as ambulances, filled with wounded, passing up Fourteenth street, on their way, probably, to Columbian, Carver, and Mount Pleasant hospitals. This is the way the men come in now, seldom in small numbers, but almost always in these long, sad processions. Through the past winter, while our army lay opposite Fredericksburg, the like strings of ambulances were of frequent occurrence along Seventh street, passing slowly up from the steamboat wharf, from Aquia creek.

This afternoon, July 22, 1863, I spent a long time with a young man I have been with considerable, named Oscar F. Wilber, Company G, One Hundred Fifty-fourth New York, low with chronic diarrhœa and a bad wound also. He

The Wound Dresser

asked me to read him a chapter in the New Testament. I complied and asked him what I should read. He said, "Make your own choice." I opened at the close of one of the first books of the Evangelists, and read the chapters describing the latter hours of Christ and the scenes at the crucifixion. The poor wasted young man asked me to read the following chapter also, how Christ rose again. I read very slowly, for Oscar was feeble. It pleased him very much, yet the tears were in his eyes. He asked me if I enjoyed religion. I said, "Perhaps not, my dear, in the way you mean, and yet may-be it is the same thing." He said, "It is my chief reliance." He talked of death, and said he did not fear it. I said, "Why, Oscar, don't you think you will get well?" He said, "I may, but it is not probable." He spoke calmly of his condition. The wound was very bad; it discharged much. Then the diarrhœa had prostrated him, and I felt that he was even then the same as dying. He behaved very manly and affectionate. The kiss I gave him as I was about leaving, he returned fourfold. He gave me his mother's address, Mrs. Sally D. Wilber, Alleghany post-office, Cattaraugus county, N. Y. I had several such interviews with him. He died a few days after the one just described.

August, September, October, etc. — I continue among the hospitals in the same manner, getting still more experience, and daily and nightly meeting with most interesting cases. Through

Hospital Visits

the winter of 1863-4, the same. The work of the army hospital visitor is indeed a trade, an art, requiring both experience and natural gifts, and the greatest judgment. A large number of the visitors to the hospitals do no good at all, while many do harm. The surgeons have great trouble from them. Some visitors go from curiosity — as to a show of animals. Others give the men improper things. Then there are always some poor fellows, in the crises of sickness or wounds, that imperatively need perfect quiet — not to be talked to by strangers. Few realize that it is not the mere giving of gifts that does good; it is the proper adaption. Nothing is of any avail among the soldiers except conscientious personal investigation of cases, each for itself; with sharp, critical faculties, but in the fullest spirit of human sympathy and boundless love. The men feel such love more than anything else. I have met very few persons who realize the importance of humoring the yearnings for love and friendship of these American young men, prostrated by sickness and wounds.

February, 1864. — I am down at Culpepper and Brandy station, among the camp of First, Second, and Third Corps, and going through the division hospitals. The condition of the camps here this winter is immensely improved from last winter near Falmouth. All the army is now in huts of logs and mud, with fireplaces; and the food is plentiful and tolerably good. In the

The Wound Dresser

camp hospitals I find diarrhœa more and more prevalent, and in chronic form. It is at present the great disease of the army. I think the doctors generally give too much medicine, oftener making things worse. Then they hold on to the cases in camp too long. When the disease is almost fixed beyond remedy, they send it up to Washington. Alas! how many such wrecks have I seen landed from boat and railroad and deposited in the Washington hospitals, mostly but to linger awhile and die, after being kept at the front too long.

The hospitals in front, this winter, are also much improved. The men have cots, and often wooden floors, and the tents are well warmed.

March and April, 1864. — Back again in Washington. They are breaking up the camp hospitals in Meade's army, preparing for a move. As I write this, in March, there are all the signs. Yesterday and last night the sick were arriving here in long trains, all day and night. I was among the new-comers most of the night. One train of a thousand came into the depot, and others followed. The ambulances were going all night, distributing them to the various hospitals here. When they come in, some literally in a dying condition, you may well imagine it is a lamentable sight. I hardly know which is worse, to see the wounded after a battle, or these wasted wrecks.

I remain in capital health and strength, and go every day, as before, among the men, in my own

Hospital Visits

way, enjoying my life and occupation more than I can tell.

Of the army hospitals now in and around Washington, there are thirty or forty. I am in the habit of going to all, and to Fairfax seminary, Alexandria, and over Long Bridge to the convalescent camp, etc. As a specimen of almost any one of these hospitals, fancy to yourself a space of three to twenty acres of ground, on which are grouped ten or twelve very large wooden barracks, with, perhaps, a dozen or twenty, and sometimes more than that number, of small buildings, capable all together of accommodating from five hundred to a thousand or fifteen hundred persons. Sometimes these large wooden barracks, or wards, each of them, perhaps, from a hundred to a hundred and fifty feet long, are arranged in a straight row, evenly fronting the street; others are planned so as to form an immense V; and others again arranged around a hollow square. They make all together a huge cluster, with the additional tents, extra wards for contagious diseases, guard-houses, sutler's stores, chaplain's house, etc. In the middle will probably be an edifice devoted to the offices of the surgeon in charge and the ward surgeons, principal attachés, clerks, etc. Then around this centre radiate or are gathered the wards for the wounded and sick.

These wards are either lettered alphabetically, Ward G, Ward K, or else numerically, 1, 2, 3, etc. Each has its ward surgeon and corps of nurses.

The Wound Dresser

Of course there is, in the aggregate, quite a muster of employees, and over all the surgeon in charge. Any one of these hospitals is a little city in itself. Take, for instance, the Carver hospital, out a couple of miles, on a hill, northern part of Fourteenth street. It has more inmates than an ordinary country town. The same with the Lincoln hospital, east of the Capitol, or the Finley hospital, on high grounds northeast of the city; both large establishments. Armory-square hospital, under Dr. Bliss, in Seventh street (one of the best anywhere), is also temporarily enlarged this summer, with additional tents, sheds, etc. It must have nearly a hundred tents, wards, sheds, and structures of one kind and another. The worst cases are always to be found here. A wanderer like me about Washington pauses on some high land which commands the sweep of the city (one never tires of the noble and ample views presented here, in the generally fine, soft, peculiar air and light), and has his eyes attracted by these white clusters of barracks in almost every direction. They make a great show in the landscape, and I often use them as landmarks. Some of these clusters are very full of inmates. Counting the whole, with the convalescent camps (whose inmates are often worse off than the sick in the hospitals), they have numbered, in this quarter and just down the Potomac, as high as fifty thousand invalid, disabled, or sick and dying men.

My sketch has already filled up so much room

Hospital Visits

that I shall have to omit any detailed account of the wounded of May and June, 1864, from the battles of the Wilderness, Spottsylvania, etc. That would be a long history in itself. The arrivals, the numbers, and the severity of the wounds, out-viewed anything that we have seen before. For days and weeks a melancholy tide set in upon us. The weather was very hot. The wounded had been delayed in coming, and much neglected. Very many of the wounds had worms in them. An unusual proportion mortified. It was among these that, for the first time in my life, I began to be prostrated with real sickness, and was, before the close of the summer, imperatively ordered North by the physician to recuperate and have an entire change of air.

What I know of first Fredericksburg, Chancellorsville, Wilderness, etc., makes clear to me that there has been, and is yet, a total lack of science in elastic adaptation to the needs of the wounded after a battle. The hospitals are long afterward filled with proofs of this.

I have seen many battles, their results, but never one where there was not, during the first few days, an unaccountable and almost total deficiency of everything for the wounded — appropriate sustenance, nursing, cleaning, medicines, stores, etc. (I do not say surgical attendance, because the surgeons cannot do more than human endurance permits.) Whatever pleasant accounts there may be in the papers of the North, this is the actual fact. No thorough previous prepara-

The Wound Dresser

tion, no system, no foresight, no genius. Always plenty of stores, no doubt, but always miles away; never where they are needed, and never the proper application. Of all harrowing experiences, none is greater than that of the days following a heavy battle. Scores, hundreds, of the noblest young men on earth, uncomplaining, lie helpless, mangled, faint, alone, and so bleed to death, or die from exhaustion, either actually untouched at all, or with merely the laying of them down and leaving them, when there ought to be means provided to save them.

The reader has doubtless inferred the fact that my visits among the wounded and sick have been as an independent missionary, in my own style, and not as an agent of any commission. Several noble women and men of Brooklyn, Boston, Salem, and Providence, have voluntarily supplied funds at times. I only wish they could see a tithe of the actual work performed by their generous and benevolent assistance among the suffering men.

He who goes among the soldiers with gifts, etc., must beware how he proceeds. It is much more of an art than one would imagine. They are not charity-patients, but American young men, of pride and independence. The spirit in which you treat them, and bestow your donations, is just as important as the gifts themselves; sometimes more so. Then there is continual discrimination necessary. Each case requires some peculiar adaptation to itself. It is very impor-

Hospital Visits

tant to slight nobody — not a single case. Some hospital visitors, especially the women, pick out the handsomest looking soldiers, or have a few for their pets. Of course some will attract you more than others, and some will need more attention than others; but be careful not to ignore any patient. A word, a friendly turn of the eye or touch of the hand in passing, if nothing more.

One hot day toward the middle of June I gave the inmates of Carver hospital a general ice-cream treat, purchasing a large quantity, and going around personally through the wards to see to its distribution.

Here is a characteristic scene in a ward: It is Sunday afternoon (middle of summer, 1864), hot and oppressive, and very silent through the ward. I am taking care of a critical case, now lying in a half lethargy. Near where I sit is a suffering Rebel from the Eighth Louisiana; his name is Irving. He has been here a long time, badly wounded, and lately had his leg amputated. It is not doing very well. Right opposite me is a sick soldier boy laid down with his clothes on, sleeping, looking much wasted, his pallid face on his arm. I see by the yellow trimming on his jacket that he is a cavalry boy. He looks so handsome as he sleeps, one must needs go nearer to him. I step softly over, and find by his card that he is named William Cone, of the First Maine Cavalry, and his folks live in Skowhegan.

Well, poor John Mahay is dead. He died yesterday. His was a painful and lingering case.

The Wound Dresser

I have been with him at times for the past fifteen months. He belonged to Company A, One Hundred and First New York, and was shot through the lower region of the abdomen at second Bull Run, August, 1862. One scene at his bedside will suffice for the agonies of nearly two years. The bladder had been perforated by a bullet going entirely through him. Not long since I sat a good part of the morning by his bedside, Ward E, Armory-square; the water ran out of his eyes from the intense pain, and the muscles of his face were distorted, but he utters nothing except a low groan now and then. Hot moist cloths were applied, and relieved him somewhat. Poor Mahay, a mere boy in age, but old in misfortune, he never knew the love of parents, was placed in his infancy in one of the New York charitable institutions, and subsequently bound out to a tyrannical master in Sullivan county (the scars of whose cowhide and club remained yet on his back). His wound here was a most disagreeable one, for he was a gentle, cleanly, and affectionate boy. He found friends in his hospital life, and, indeed, was a universal favorite. He had quite a funeral ceremony.

Through Fourteenth street to the river, and then over the long bridge and some three miles beyond, is the huge collection called the convalescent camp. It is a respectable sized army in itself, for these hospitals, tents, sheds, etc., at times contain from five to ten thousand men. Of course there are continual changes. Large

Hospital Visits

squads are sent off to their regiments or elsewhere, and new men received. Sometimes I found large numbers of paroled returned prisoners here.

During October, November, and December, 1864, I have visited the military hospitals about New York City, but have not room in this article to describe these visits.

I have lately been (November 25) in the Central-park hospital, near One Hundred and Fourth street; it seems to be a well-managed institution. During September, and previously, went many times to the Brooklyn city hospital, in Raymond street, where I found (taken in by contract) a number of wounded and sick from the army. Most of the men were badly off, and without a cent of money, many wanting tobacco. I supplied them, and a few special cases with delicacies; also repeatedly with letter-paper, stamps, envelopes, etc., writing the addresses myself plainly — (a pleased crowd gathering around me as I directed for each one in turn.) This Brooklyn hospital is a bad place for soldiers, or anybody else. Cleanliness, proper nursing, watching, etc., are more deficient than in any hospital I know. For dinner on Sundays I invariably found nothing but rice and molasses. The men all speak well of Drs. Yale and Kissam for kindness, patience, etc., and I think, from what I saw, there are also young medical men. In its management otherwise, this is the poorest hospital I have been in, out of many hundreds.

Among places, apart from soldiers', visited

The Wound Dresser

lately (December 7) I must specially mention the great Brooklyn general hospital and other public institutions at Flatbush, including the extensive lunatic asylum, under charge of Drs. Chapin and Reynolds. Of the latter (and I presume I might include these county establishments generally) I have deliberately to put on record about the profoundest satisfaction with professional capacity, completeness of house arrangements to ends required, and the right vital spirit animating all, that I have yet found in any public curative institution among civilians.

In Washington, in camp and everywhere, I was in the habit of reading to the men. They were very fond of it, and liked declamatory, poetical pieces. Miles O'Reilly's pieces were also great favorites. I have had many happy evenings with the men. We would gather in a large group by ourselves, after supper, and spend the time in such readings, or in talking, and occasionally by an amusing game called the game of Twenty Questions.

For nurses, middle-aged women and mothers of families are best. I am compelled to say young ladies, however refined, educated, and benevolent, do not succeed as army nurses, though their motives are noble; neither do the Catholic nuns, among these home-born American young men. Mothers full of motherly feeling, and however illiterate, but bringing reminiscences of home, and with the magnetic touch of hands, are the true women nurses. Many of the

Hospital Visits

wounded are between fifteen and twenty years of age.

I should say that the Government, from my observation, is always full of anxiety and liberality toward the sick and wounded. The system in operation in the permanent hospitals is good, and the money flows without stint. But the details have to be left to hundreds and thousands of subordinates and officials. Among these, laziness, heartlessness, gouging, and incompetency are more or less prevalent. Still, I consider the permanent hospitals, generally, well conducted.

A very large proportion of the wounded come up from the front without a cent of money in their pockets. I soon discovered that it was about the best thing I could do to raise their spirits and show them that somebody cared for them, and practically felt a fatherly or brotherly interest in them, to give them small sums, in such cases, using tact and discretion about it.

A large majority of the wounds are in the arms and legs. But there is every kind of wound in every part of the body. I should say of the sick, from my experience in the hospitals, that the prevailing maladies are typhoid fever and the camp fevers generally, diarrhœa, catarrhal affections and bronchitis, rheumatism and pneumonia. These forms of sickness lead, all the rest follow. There are twice as many sick as there are wounded. The deaths range from six to ten per cent of those under treatment.

I must bear my most emphatic testimony to

The Wound Dresser

the zeal, manliness, and professional spirit and capacity generally prevailing among the surgeons, many of them young men, in the hospitals and the army. I will not say much about the exceptions, for they are few (but I have met some of those few, and very foolish and airish they were). I never ceased to find the best young men, and the hardest and most disinterested workers, among these surgeons, in the hospitals. They are full of genius, too. I have seen many hundreds of them, and this is my testimony.

During my two years in the hospitals and upon the field, I have made over six hundred visits, and have been, as I estimate, among from eighty thousand to one hundred thousand of the wounded and sick, as sustainer of spirit and body in some slight degree, in their time of need. These visits varied from an hour or two, to all day or night; for with dear or critical cases I watched all night. Sometimes I took up my quarters in the hospital, and slept or watched there several nights in succession. I may add that I am now just resuming my occupation in the hospitals and camps for the winter of 1864-5, and probably to continue the seasons ensuing.

To many of the wounded and sick, especially the youngsters, there is something in personal love, caresses, and the magnetic flood of sympathy and friendship, that does, in its way, more good than all the medicine in the world. I have spoken of my regular gifts of delicacies, money, tobacco, special articles of food, knick-knacks,

Hospital Visits

etc., etc. But I steadily found more and more that I could help, and turn the balance in favor of cure, by the means here alluded to, in a curiously large proportion of cases. The American soldier is full of affection and the yearning for affection. And it comes wonderfully grateful to him to have this yearning gratified when he is laid up with painful wounds or illness, far away from home, among strangers. Many will think this merely sentimentalism, but I know it is the most solid of facts. I believe that even the moving around among the men, or through the ward, of a hearty, healthy, clean, strong, generous-souled person, man or woman, full of humanity and love, sending out invisible, constant currents thereof, does immense good to the sick and wounded.

To those who might be interested in knowing it, I must add, in conclusion, that I have tried to do justice to all the suffering that fell in my way. While I have been with wounded and sick in thousands of cases from the New England States, and from New York, New Jersey, and Pennsylvania, and from Michigan, Wisconsin, Indiana, Illinois, and the Western States, I have been with more or less from all the States North and South, without exception. I have been with many from the border States, especially from Maryland and Virginia, and found far more Union Southerners than is supposed. I have been with many Rebel officers and men among our wounded, and given them always what I had, and tried to cheer them

The Wound Dresser

the same as any. I have been among the army teamsters considerably, and indeed always find myself drawn to them. Among the black soldiers, wounded or sick, and in the contraband camps, I also took my way whenever in their neighborhood, and I did what I could for them.

W. W.

From the New York Times, *December 11, 1864.*

LOUISA (VAN VELSOR) WHITMAN
From a Daguerreotype taken about 1855

LETTERS OF 1862-3

I

WASHINGTON, *Monday forenoon, Dec. 29, 1862.* DEAR, DEAR MOTHER — Friday the 19th inst. I succeeded in reaching the camp of the 51st New York, and found George[1] alive and well. In order to make sure that you would get the good news, I sent back by messenger to Washington a telegraphic dispatch (I dare say you did not get it for some time) as well as a letter — and the same to Hannah[2] at Burlington. I have staid in camp with George ever since, till yesterday, when I came back to Washington, about the 24th. George got Jeff's[3] letter of the 20th. Mother, how much you must have suffered, all that week, till George's letter came — and all the rest must too. As to me, I know I put in about three days of the greatest suffering I ever experienced in my life. I wrote to Jeff how I had my pocket picked in a jam and hurry, changing cars, at Philadelphia — so that I landed here without a dime. The next two days I spent hunting through the hospitals, walking day and night, unable to ride, trying to get information —

[1] His brother, Capt. (afterwards Col.) George W. Whitman, born 1829, now (1897) residing in Burlington, N. J.
[2] His favorite sister, Hannah Louisa Whitman (Mrs. C. L. Heyde), born 1823, now (1897) residing in Burlington, Vt.
[3] His brother, Thomas Jefferson Whitman, born 1833, died 1890.

The Wound Dresser

trying to get access to big people, etc. — I could not get the least clue to anything. Odell would not see me at all. But Thursday afternoon, I lit on a way to get down on the Government boat that runs to Aquia creek, and so by railroad to the neighborhood of Falmouth, opposite Fredericksburg — so by degrees I worked my way to Ferrero's[1] brigade, which I found Friday afternoon without much trouble after I got in camp. When I found dear brother George, and found that he was alive and well, O you may imagine how trifling all my little cares and difficulties seemed — they vanished into nothing. And now that I have lived for eight or nine days amid such scenes as the camps furnish, and had a practical part in it all, and realize the way that hundreds of thousands of good men are now living, and have had to live for a year or more, not only without any of the comforts, but with death and sickness and hard marching and hard fighting (and no success at that) for their continual experience — really nothing we call trouble seems worth talking about. One of the first things that met my eyes in camp was a heap of feet, arms, legs, etc., under a tree in front of a hospital, the Lacy house.

George is very well in health, has a good appetite — I think he is at times more wearied out

---

[1] Brig.-Gen. Edward Ferrero, commanding Second Brigade, Second Division, Army of the Potomac, under whose command the 51st Brooklyn Regiment fought at Fredericksburg. George Whitman was a captain in this regiment.

Letters of 1862-3

and homesick than he shows, but stands it upon the whole very well. Every one of the soldiers, to a man, wants to get home.

I suppose Jeff got quite a long letter I wrote, from camp, about a week ago. I told you that George had been promoted to captain — his commission arrived while I was there. When you write, address, Capt. George W. Whitman, Co. K., 51st New York Volunteers, Ferrero's brigade, near Falmouth, Va. Jeff must write oftener, and put in a few lines from mother, even if it is only two lines — then in the next letter a few lines from Mat, and so on. You have no idea how letters from home cheer one up in camp, and dissipate homesickness.

While I was there George still lived in Capt. Francis's tent — there were five of us altogether, to eat, sleep, write, etc., in a space twelve feet square, but we got along very well — the weather all along was very fine — and would have got along to perfection, but Capt. Francis is not a man I could like much — I had very little to say to him. George is about building a place, half hut and half tent, for himself, (he is probably about it this very day,) and then he will be better off, I think. Every captain has a tent, in which he lives, transacts company business, etc., has a cook, (or a man of all work,) and in the same tent mess and sleep his lieutenants, and perhaps the first sergeant. They have a kind of fire-place — and the cook's fire is outside on the open ground. George had very good times while Francis was

The Wound Dresser

away — the cook, a young disabled soldier, Tom, is an excellent fellow and a first-rate cook, and the second lieutenant, Pooley, is a tip-top young Pennsylvanian. Tom thinks all the world of George; when he heard he was wounded, on the day of the battle, he left everything, got across the river, and went hunting for George through the field, through thick and thin. I wrote to Jeff that George was wounded by a shell, a gash in the cheek — you could stick a splint through into the mouth, but it has healed up without difficulty already. Everything is uncertain about the army, whether it moves or stays where it is. There are no furloughs granted at present. I will stay here for the present, at any rate long enough to see if I can get any employment at anything, and shall write what luck I have. Of course I am unsettled at present. Dear mother, my love. WALT.

If Jeff or any writes, address me, care of Major Hapgood, paymaster, U. S. A. Army, Washington, D. C. I send my love to dear sister Mat,[1] and little Sis[2] — and to Andrew[3] and all

---

[1] Martha, wife of "Jeff." She died in 1873. "1873. — This year lost, by death, my dear dear mother — and just before, my sister Martha — the two best and sweetest women I have ever seen or known, or ever expect to see" (WALT WHITMAN, "Some Personal and Old Age Jottings").

[2] "Jeff's" little daughter, Mannahatta. She died in 1888.

[3] His brother, Andrew Jackson Whitman, born 1827, died 1863. His other brothers at this time, besides those previously mentioned, were Jesse Whitman, born 1818, died 1870, and Edward Whitman, born 1835, died 1892.

Letters of 1862-3

my brothers. O Mat, how lucky it was you did not come — together, we could never have got down to see George.

II

Washington, Friday morning, Jan. 2, 1863.
DEAR SISTER[1] — You have heard of my fortunes and misfortunes of course, (through my letters to mother and Jeff,) since I left home that Tuesday afternoon. But I thought I would write a few lines to you, as it is a comfort to write home, even if I have nothing particular to say. Well, dear sister, I hope you are well and hearty, and that little Sis[2] keeps as well as she always had, when I left home so far. Dear little plague, how I would like to have her with me, for one day; I can fancy I see her, and hear her talk. Jeff must have got a note from me about a letter I have written to the *Eagle* — you may be sure you will get letters enough from me, for I have little else to do at present. Since I laid my eyes on dear brother George, and saw him alive and well — and since I have spent a week in camp, down there opposite Fredericksburg, and seen what well men, and sick men, and mangled men endure — it seems to me I can be satisfied and happy henceforward if I can get one meal a day, and know that mother and all are in good health, and especially be with

[1] Martha.
[2] Mannahatta.

The Wound Dresser

you again, and have some little steady paying occupation in N. Y. or Brooklyn.

I am writing this in the office of Major Hapgood, way up in the top of a big high house, corner of 15th and F street; there is a splendid view, away down south of the Potomac river, and across to the Georgetown side, and the grounds and houses of Washington spread out beneath my high point of view. The weather is perfect — I have had that in my favor ever since leaving home — yesterday and to-day it is bright, and plenty warm enough. The poor soldiers are continually coming in from the hospitals, etc., to get their pay — some of them waiting for it to go home. They climb up here, quite exhausted, and then find it is no good, for there is no money to pay them; there are two or three paymasters' desks in this room, and the scenes of disappointment are quite affecting. Here they wait in Washington, perhaps week after week, wretched and heart-sick — this is the greatest place of delays and puttings off, and no finding the clue to anything. This building is the paymaster-general's quarters, and the crowds on the walk and corner of poor, sick, pale, tattered soldiers are awful — many of them day after day disappointed and tired out. Well, Mat, I will suspend my letter for the present, and go through the city — I have a couple of poor fellows in the hospital to visit also. WALT.

Saturday evening, Jan. 3 [1863.] I write this in the place where I have my lodging-room, 394

Letters of 1862-3

L street, 4th door above 14th street. A friend of mine, William D. O'Connor,[1] has two apartments on the 3rd floor, very ordinarily furnished, for which he pays the *extra*ordinary price of $25 a month. I have a werry little bedroom on the 2nd floor. Mr. and Mrs. O'Connor and their little girl have all gone out "down town" for an hour or two, to make some Saturday evening purchases, and I am left in possession of the premises — so I sit by the fire, and scribble more of my letter. I have not heard anything from dear brother George since I left the camp last Sunday morning, 28th Dec. I wrote to him on Tuesday last. I wish to get to him the two blue woolen shirts Jeff sent, as they would come very acceptable to him — and will try to do it yet. I think of sending them by mail, if the postage is not more than $1.

Yesterday I went out to the Campbell hospital to see a couple of Brooklyn boys, of the 51st. They knew I was in Washington, and sent me a note, to come and see them. O my dear sister, how your heart would ache to go through the rows of wounded young men, as I did — and stopt to speak a comforting word to them. There were about 100 in one long room, just a long shed neatly whitewashed inside. One young man was very much prostrated, and groaning with

---

[1] William Douglas O'Connor, born Jan. 2, 1832. He was a journalist in Boston in early life, went to Washington about 1861, first as clerk in the Light House Bureau, and later became Assistant Superintendent of the United States Life-Saving Service; died in Washington, May 9, 1889. He was one of Whitman's warmest friends, and the author of "The Good Gray Poet."

The Wound Dresser

pain. I stopt and tried to comfort him. He was very sick. I found he had not had any medical attention since he was brought there; among so many he had been overlooked; so I sent for the doctor, and he made an examination of him. The doctor behaved very well — seemed to be anxious to do right — said that the young man would recover; he had been brought pretty low with diarrhœa, and now had bronchitis, but not so serious as to be dangerous. I talked to him some time — he seemed to have entirely given up, and lost heart — he had not a cent of money — not a friend or acquaintance. I wrote a letter from him to his sister — his name is John A. Holmes, Campello, Plymouth county, Mass. I gave him a little change I had — he said he would like to buy a drink of milk when the woman came through with milk. Trifling as this was, he was overcome and began to cry. Then there were many, many others. I mention the one, as a specimen. My Brooklyn boys were John Lowery, shot at Fredericksburg, and lost his left forearm, and Amos H. Vliet — Jeff knows the latter — he has his feet frozen, and is doing well. The 100 are in a ward, (6), and there are, I should think, eight or ten or twelve such wards in the Campbell hospital — indeed a real village. Then there are 38 more hospitals here in Washington, some of them much larger.

Sunday forenoon, Jan. 4, 1863. Mat, I hope and trust dear mother and all are well, and everything goes on good home. The envelope I send, Jeff

Letters of 1862-3

or any of you can keep for direction, or use it when wanted to write to me. As near as I can tell, the army at Falmouth remains the same. Dear sister, good-bye. WALT.

I send my love to Andrew and Jesse and Eddy and all. What distressing news this is of the loss of the Monitor.[1]

III

Washington, Friday noon, February 6, 1863. DEAREST MOTHER — Jeff must have got a letter from me yesterday, containing George's last letter. The news of your sickness and the strange silence of Han made me feel somewhat gloomy. I wrote to George yesterday, conveying the news — and to-day I have sent him another letter, with much more comforting news, for I was so glad to hear from Han (her letter enclosed in Jeff's received this morning) that I wrote him right away, and sent Han's letter.

Mother, I am quite in hopes George will get a furlough — may-be my expectations are unfounded, but I almost count on it. I am so glad this morning to hear you are no worse, but changed for the better — and dear sister Mat too, and Sissy, I am so glad to think they are recovering. Jeff's enclosure of $10 through Mr. Lane, from the young engineers for the soldiers

---

[1] The Monitor foundered off Cape Hatteras in a gale December 29, 1862.

The Wound Dresser

in hospitals, the most needy cases, came safe of course — I shall acknowledge it to Mr. Lane tomorrow. Mother, I have written so much about hospitals that I will not write any in this letter.

We have had bad weather enough here lately to most make up for the delightful weather we had for five weeks after I came from home.

Mother, I do hope you will be careful, and not get any relapse — and hope you will go on improving. Do you then think of getting new apartments, after the 1st of May? I suppose Jeff has settled about the lot — it seems to me first rate as an investment — the kind of house to build is quite a consideration (if any house). I should build a *regular Irish shanty* myself — two rooms, and an end shed. I think that's luxury enough, since I have been down in the army.

Well, mother, I believe I will not fill out the sheet this time, as I want to go down without delay to the P. O. and send George's letter and this one. Good-bye, dear mother. WALT.

IV

Washington, Monday morning, Feb. 9, 1863.
DEAREST MOTHER — I write to enclose you a letter I have just received from George. His corps (Ninth Army) and perhaps one other are to move either to Fort Monroe, or somewhere down there — some say Suffolk. I am in hopes

Letters of 1862-3

that when they get there, George will still have a sight for a furlough. I have written him I should think four letters since the 27th Jan. (and have sent him Han's letter to you in one). I hope he has got most of them before this. I am afraid the $3 change I sent him is gone. He will write to you as soon as he gets settled wherever they go to. I don't know as it makes any difference in respect to danger, or fighting, from this move. One reason they have to move from the Rappahannock, up there, is that wood is all gone for miles, forage is scarce to get, and I don't know as there is any need of their staying there, for any purpose. In some haste, dearest mother, as I am off to visit for an hour or so, one of my hospitals. Your affectionate son, WALT.

V

Office Major Hapgood, cor. 15th & F sts, Washington, Feb. 13, 1863. DEAR BROTHER[1] — Nothing new; still I thought I would write you a line this morning. The $4, namely $2 from Theo A. Drake and $2 from John D. Martin, enclosed in your letter of the 10th, came safe. They too will please accept the grateful thanks of several poor fellows, in hospital here.

The letter of introduction to Mr. Webster, chief clerk, State department, will be very acceptable. If convenient, I should like Mr.

[1] "Jeff."

The Wound Dresser

Lane to send it on immediately. I do not so much look for an appointment from Mr. Seward as his backing me from the State of New York. I have seen Preston King this morning for the second time (it is very amusing to hunt for an office — so the thing seems to me just now, even if one don't get it). I have seen Charles Sumner three times — he says ev'ry thing here moves as part of a great machine, and that I must consign myself to the fate of the rest — still [in] an interview I had with him yesterday he talked and acted as though he had life in him, and would exert himself to any reasonable extent for me to get something. Meantime I make about enough to pay my expenses by hacking on the press here, and copying in the paymasters' offices, a couple of hours a day. One thing is favorable here, namely, pay for whatever one does is at a high rate. I have not yet presented my letters to either Seward or Chase — I thought I would get my forces all in a body, and make one concentrated dash, if possible with the personal introduction and presence of some big bug. I like fat old Preston King very much — he is fat as a hogshead, with great hanging chops. The first thing he said to me the other day in the parlor chambers of the Senate, when I sent in for him and he came out, was, "Why, how can I do this thing, or any thing for you — how do I know but you are a Secessionist? You look for all the world like an old Southern planter — a regular Carolina or

Letters of 1862-3

Virginia planter." I treated him with just as much hauteur as he did me with bluntness — this was the first time — it afterward proved that Charles Sumner had not prepared the way for me, as I supposed, or rather not so strongly as I supposed, and Mr. King had even forgotten it — so I was an entire stranger. But the same day C. S. talked further with Mr. King in the Senate, and the second interview I had with the latter (this forenoon) he has given me a sort of general letter, endorsing me from New York — one envelope is addressed to Secretary Chase, and another to Gen. Meigs, head Quartermaster's dept. Meantime, I am getting better and better acquainted with office-hunting wisdom and Washington peculiarities generally. I spent several hours in the Capitol the other day. The incredible gorgeousness of some of the rooms, (interior decorations, etc.) — rooms used perhaps but for merely three or four committee meetings in the course of the whole year — is beyond one's flightiest dreams. Costly frescoes of the style of Taylor's saloon in Broadway, only really the best and choicest of their sort, done by imported French and Italian artists, are the prevailing sorts. (Imagine the work you see on the fine china vases in Tiffany's, the paintings of Cupids and goddesses, etc., spread recklessly over the arched ceiling and broad panels of a big room — the whole floor underneath paved with tesselated pavement, which is a sort of cross between marble and china, with little figures, drab, blue, cream color, etc.)

The Wound Dresser

These things, with heavy elaborately wrought balustrades, columns, and steps — all of the most beautiful marbles I ever saw, some white as milk, other of all colors, green, spotted, lined, or of our old chocolate color — all these marbles used as freely as if they were common blue flags — with rich door-frames and window-casings of bronze and gold — heavy chandeliers and mantles, and clocks in every room — and indeed by far the richest and gayest, and most un-American and inappropriate ornamenting and finest interior workmanship I ever conceived possible, spread in profusion through scores, hundreds, (and almost thousands) of rooms — such are what I find, or rather would find to interest me, if I devoted time to it. But a few of the rooms are enough for me — the style is without grandeur, and without simplicity. These days, the state our country is in, and especially filled as I am from top to toe of late with scenes and thoughts of the hospitals, (America seems to me now, though only in her youth, but brought already here, feeble, bandaged, and bloody in hospital) — these days I say, Jeff, all the poppy-show goddesses, and all the pretty blue and gold in which the interior Capitol is got up, seem to me out of place beyond anything I could tell — and I get away from it as quick as I can when that kind of thought comes over me. I suppose it is to be described throughout — those interiors — as all of them got up in the French style — well, enough for a New York.

Letters of 1862-3
VI

Washington, March 31, 1863. DEAREST MOTHER — I have not heard from George, except a note he wrote me a couple of days after he got back from his furlough. I think it likely the regiment has gone with its corps to the West, the Kentucky or Tennessee region — Burnside at last accounts was in Cincinnati. Well, it will be a change for George, if he is out there. I sent a long letter to Han last Saturday — enclosed George's note to me. Mother, when you or Jeff writes again, tell me if my papers and MSS. are all right; I should be very sorry indeed if they got scattered, or used up or anything — especially the copy of "Leaves of Grass" covered in blue paper,[1] and the little MS. book "Drum-Taps," and the MS. tied up in the square, spotted (stone-paper) loose covers — I want them all carefully kept.

Mother, it is quite a snow-storm here this morning — the ground is an inch and a half deep with snow — and it is snowing and drizzling — but I feel very independent in my stout army-boots; I go anywhere. I *have* felt quite well

---

[1] A copy of the 1860 (first Boston) edition of "Leaves of Grass," which Whitman used for preparing the next (1867) edition. From various evidence this is the same copy, with his MS. alterations, which Secretary Harlan found in Whitman's desk at the Interior Department in 1865, and which he read surreptitiously before discharging the poet from his position. It is now in the possession of Mr. Horace L. Traubel, of Camden, N. J.

The reference to "Drum-Taps," published in 1865, shows that it had already taken shape in MS.

The Wound Dresser

of my deafness and cold in my head for four days or so, but it is back again bad as ever this morning.

Dear mother, I wrote the above in my room — I have now come down to Major Hapgood's office. I do not find anything from home, and no particular news in the paper this morning — no news about the Ninth Army Corps, or where they are. I find a good letter from one of my New York boys, (Fifth avenue) a young fellow named Hugo Fritsch, son of the Austrian Consul-General — he writes me a long, first-rate letter this morning. He too speaks about the Opera — like Jeff he goes there a good deal — says that Medori, the soprano, as Norma made the greatest success ever seen — says that the whole company there now, the singers, are very fine. All this I write for Jeff and Mat — I hope they will go once in a while when it is convenient.

It is a most disagreeable day here, mother, walking poshy and a rain and drizzle.

There is nothing new with me, no particular sight for an office that I can count on. But I can make enough with the papers, for the present necessities. I hear that the paymaster, Major Yard, that pays the 51st, has gone on West, I suppose to Cincinnati, or wherever the brigade has gone — of course to pay up — he pays up to 1st of March — all the Army is going to be paid up to 1st March everywhere.

Mother, I hope you are well and hearty as usual. I am so glad you are none of you going

Letters of 1862-3

to move. I would like to have the pleasure of Miss Mannahatta Whitman's company, the first fine forenoon, if it were possible; I think we might have first-rate times, for one day at any rate. I hope she will not forget her Uncle Walt. I received a note from Probasco, requesting me not to put his name in my next letter. I appreciate his motive, and wish to please him always—but in this matter I shall do what I think appropriate. Mother, I see some very interesting persons here—a young master's mate, who was on the Hatteras, when surprised and broadsided by the Alabama, Capt Semmes—he gave me a very good acc't of it all—then Capt. Mullen, U. S. Army, (engineer) who has been six years out in the Rocky mts. making a Gov't road 650 miles from Ft. Benton to Walla Walla —very, very interesting to know such men intimately, and talk freely with them. Dearest mother, I shall have great yarns to spin, when I come home. I am not a bit homesick, yet I should like to see you and Mat very, very much —one thinks of the women when he is away.

WALT.

Shall send the shirts in a day or two.

VII

Washington, Wednesday forenoon, April 15, 1863.
DEAREST MOTHER — Jeff's letter of the 11th, acknowledging the books, also the one about five days previous, containing the $10 from Van

The Wound Dresser

Anden, came safe. Jeff's letters are always first rate and welcome — the good long one with so much about home, and containing Han's and George's, was especially so. It is a great pleasure, though sometimes a melancholy one, to hear from Han, under her own hand. I have writ to George — I wrote last Friday. I directed the letter to "Lexington or elsewhere, Kentucky"— as I saw in a letter in a Cincinnati paper that Gen. Ferrero was appointed provost marshal at Lexington. The 51st is down there somewhere, and I guess it is about as well off there as anywhere. There is much said about their closing up the regimental companies — that is, where there are ten companies of 40 men each, closing them up to five companies, of 80 men each. It is said the Government purposes something of this kind. It will throw a good many captains and lieutenants out. I suppose you know that Le Gendre is now colonel of the 51st — it's a pity if we have n't Americans enough to put over our old war regiments. (I think less and less of foreigners, in this war. What I see, especially in the hospitals, convinces me that there is no other stock, for emergencies, but native American — no other name by which we can be saved.)

Mother, I feel quite bad about Andrew — I am so in hopes to hear that he has recovered — I think about him every day. He must not get fretting and disheartened — that is really the worst feature of any sickness. Diseases of the throat and bronchia are the result always of bad state of

Letters of 1862-3

the stomach, blood, etc. (they never come from the throat itself). The throat and the bronchia are lined, like the stomach and other interior organs, with a fine lining like silk or crape, and when all this gets ulcerated or inflamed or whatnot (it is Dr. Sammis's *mucous membrane*, you know) it is bad, and most distressing. Medicine is really of no great account, except just to pacify a person. This lining I speak of is full of little blood vessels, and the way to make a *real cure* is by gentle and steady means to recuperate the whole system; this will tell upon the blood, upon the blood vessels, and so finally and effectually upon all this coating I speak of that lines the throat, etc. But as it is a long time before this vital lining membrane (*very important*) is injured, so it is a long time before it can be made all healthy and right again; but Andrew is young and strong enough and [has a] good constitution for basis — and of course by regular diet, care, (and nary whiskey under any circumstances) I am sure he would not only get over that trouble, but be as well and strong as he ever was in his life. Mother, you tell him I sent him my love, and Nancy[1] the same, and the dear little boys the same — the next time you or Mat goes down there you take this and show him.

Mat, I am quite glad to hear that you are not hurried and fretted with work from New York this spring — I am sure I should think Sis and housekeeping, etc., would be enough to attend to.

[1] Andrew Whitman's wife.

The Wound Dresser

I was real amused with Sis's remarks, and all that was in the letter about her. You must none of you notice her smartness, nor criticisms, before her, nor encourage her to spread herself nor be critical, as it is not good to encourage a child to be too sharp — and I hope Sissy is going to be a splendid specimen of good animal health. For the few years to come I should think more of that than anything — that is the foundation of all (righteousness included); as to her mental vivacity and growth, they are plenty enough of themselves, and will get along quite fast enough of themselves, plenty fast enough — don't stimulate them at all. Dear little creature, how I should like to see her this minute. Jeff must not make his lessons to her in music anyways strong or frequent on any account — two lessons a week, of ten minutes each, is enough — but then I dare say Jeff will think of all these things, just the same as I am saying. Jeff writes he wonders if I am as well and hearty, and I suppose he means as much of a beauty as ever, whether I look the same. Well, not only as much but more so — I believe I weigh about 200, and as to my face, (so scarlet,) and my beard and neck, they are terrible to behold. I fancy the reason I am able to do some good in the hospitals among the poor languishing and wounded boys, is, that I am so large and well — indeed like a great wild buffalo, with much hair. Many of the soldiers are from the West, and far North, and they take to a man that has not the bleached shiny and shaved cut

Letters of 1862-3

of the cities and the East. I spent three to four hours yesterday in Armory hospital. One of my particular boys there was dying — pneumonia — he wanted me to stop with him awhile; he could not articulate — but the look of his eyes, and the holding on of his hand was deeply affecting. His case is a relapse — eight days ago he had recovered, was up, was perhaps a little careless — at any rate took cold, was taken down again and has sank rapidly. He has no friends or relatives here. Yesterday he labored and panted so for breath, it was terrible. He is a young man from New England, from the country. I expected to see his cot vacated this afternoon or evening, as I shall go down then. Mother, if you or Mat was here a couple of days, you would cry your eyes out. I find I have to restrain myself and keep my composure — I succeed pretty well. Goodbye, dearest mother. WALT.

Jeff, Capt. Muller remains here yet for some time. He is bringing out his report. I shall try to send you a copy. Give my best respects to Dr. Ruggles.

Mother, my last letter home was a week ago to-day — we are having a dark rainy day here — it is now half-past 3. I have been in my room all day so far — shall have dinner in half an hour, and then down to Armory.

The Wound Dresser

VIII

Washington, April 28, 1863. DEAREST MOTHER — A letter from Jeff came this morning. Mother, I was sorry to hear you had a return of your rheumatism — I do hope you will favor yourself more, it depends so much on that — and rheumatism is so obstinate, when it gets hold of one. Mother, you received a letter from me sent last Wednesday, 22nd, of course, with a small quantity of shinplasters. Next time you or Jeff writes, I wish you would tell me whether the letters come pretty regularly, the next morning after I write them — this now ought to reach you Wednesday forenoon, April 29th. Mother, did a Mr. Howell call on you? He was here last week to see about his boy, died a long while ago in hospital in Yorktown. He works in the Navy Yard — knows Andrew. You will see about him (the boy) in a letter I sent yesterday to the *Eagle* — it ought to appear to-day or to-morrow.

Jeff, I wish you would take 10¢ I send in this letter and get me ten copies of the *Eagle* with it in — put in five more of my pictures (the big ones in last edition " Leaves "), and a couple of the photographs carte visites (the smaller ones), and send me to the same direction as before; it came very well. I will send an *Eagle* to Han and George. The stamps and 10¢ are for Jeff for the papers and postage.

Letters of 1862-3

I have written to Han, and sent her George's last two letters from Kentucky; one I got last week from Mount Sterling. I write to George and send him papers. Sam Beatty is here in Washington again. I saw him, and he said he would write to George. Mother, I have not got any new clothes yet, but shall very soon I hope. People are more rough and free and easy drest than your way. Then it is dusty or muddy most of the time here. Mother dear, I hope you have comfortable times — at least as comfortable as the law allows. I am so glad you are not going to have the trouble of moving this 1st of May. How are the Browns? Tell Will I should like to see him first rate — if he was here attached to the suite of some big officer, or something of that kind, he would have a good time and do well. I see lots of young fellows not half as capable and trustworthy as he, coming and going in Washington, in such positions. The big generals and head men all through the armies, and provosts etc., like to have a squad of such smart, nimble young men around them. Give my respects to Mr. and Mrs. Brown.

Tell Jeff I am going to write to Mr. Lane either to-day or to-morrow. Jeff asks me if I go to hospitals as much as ever. If my letters home don't show it, you don't get 'em. I feel sorry sometimes after I have sent them, I have said so much about hospitals, and so mournful. O mother, the young man in Armory-square, Dennis Barrett, in the 169th N. Y., I mentioned

The Wound Dresser

before, is probably going to get up after all; he is like one saved from the grave. Saturday last I saw him and talked with him and gave him something to eat, and he was much better — it is the most unexpected recovery I have yet seen. Mother, I see Jeff says in the letter you don't hear from me very often — I will write oftener, especially to Jeff. Dear brother, I hope you are getting along good, and in good spirits; you must not mind the failure of the sewer bills, etc. It don't seem to me it makes so much difference about worldly successes (beyond just enough to eat and drink and shelter, in the moderatest limits) any more, since the last four months of my life especially, and that merely to live, and have one fair meal a day, is enough — but then you have a family, and that makes a difference.

Matty, I send you my best love, dear sister — how I wish I could be with you one or two good days. Mat, do you remember the good time we had that awful stormy night we went to the Opera, New York, and had the front seat, and heard the handsome-mouthed Guerrabella? and had the good oyster supper at Fulton market — ("pewter them ales.") O Mat, I hope and trust we shall have such times again.

Tell Andrew he must remember what I wrote about the throat, etc. I am sure he will get all right before long, and recover his voice. Give him my love — and tell Mannahatta her Uncle Walt is living now among the sick soldiers. Jeff, look out for the *Eagles,* and send the portraits.

Letters of 1862-3

Dearest mother, I must bid you and all for the present good-bye. WALT.

IX

Washington, Tuesday, May 5, 1863. DEAREST MOTHER — Your letter came safe, and was very welcome, and always will be. Mother, I am sorry about your rheumatism — if it still continues I think it would be well for me to write a line to Mrs. Piercy, and get Jeff to stop with it, so that you could take the baths again, as I am sure they are very beneficial. Dear mother, you write me, or Jeff must in the next letter, how you are getting along, whether it is any better or worse — I want to know. Mother, about George's fund in the bank; I hope by all means you can scratch along so as to leave $250 there — I am so anxious that our family should have a little ranch, even if it is the meanest kind, off somewhere that you can call your own, and that would do for Ed etc. — it might be a real dependence, and comfort — and may-be for George as much as any one. I mean to come home one of these days, and get the acre or half acre somewhere out in some by-place on Long Island, and build it — you see if I don't. About Hannah, dear mother, I hardly know what advice to give you — from what I know at present I can't tell what course to pursue. I want Han to come home, from the bottom of my heart. Then there are other

The Wound Dresser

thoughts and considerations that come up. Dear mother, I cannot advise, but shall acquiesce in anything that is settled upon, and try to help.

The condition of things here in the hospitals is getting pretty bad — the wounded from the battles around Fredericksburg are coming up in large numbers. It is very sad to see them. I have written to Mr. Lane, asking him to get his friends to forward me what they think proper — but somehow I feel delicate about sending such requests, after all.

I have almost made up my mind to do what I can personally, and not seek assistance from others.

Dear mother, I have not received any letter from George. I write to him and send papers to Winchester. Mother, while I have been writing this a very large number of Southern prisoners, I should think 1,000 at least, has past up Pennsylvania avenue, under a strong guard. I went out in the street, close to them. Poor fellows, many of them mere lads — it brought the tears; they seemed our flesh and blood too, some wounded, all miserable in clothing, all in dirt and tatters — many of them fine young men. Mother, I cannot tell you how I feel to see those prisoners marched.

X

Washington, Wednesday forenoon, May 13, 1863. DEAREST MOTHER — I am late with my

Letters of 1862-3

letter this week — my poor, poor boys occupy my time very much — I go every day, and sometimes nights. I believe I mentioned a young man in Ward F, Armory-square, with a bad wound in the leg, very agonizing — had to have it propt up, and an attendant all the while dripping water on night and day. I was in hopes at one time he would get through with it, but a few days ago he took a sudden bad turn and died about 3 o'clock the same afternoon — it was horrible. He was of good family — handsome, intelligent man, about 26, married; his name was John Elliot, of Cumberland Valley, Bedford co., Penn. — belonged to 2nd Pennsylvania Cavalry. I felt very bad about it. I have wrote to his father — have not received any answer yet; no friend nor any of his folks was here, and have not been here nor sent — probably don't know of it at all. The surgeons put off amputating the leg, he was so exhausted, but at last it was imperatively necessary to amputate. Mother, I am shocked to tell you that he never came alive off the amputating table — he died under the operation — it was what I had dreaded and anticipated. Poor young man, he suffered much, very, *very* much, for many days, and bore it so patiently — so that it was a release to him. Mother, such things are awful — not a soul here he knew or cared about, except me — yet the surgeons and nurses were good to him. I think all was done for him that could be — there was no help but take off the leg; he was under chloroform — they tried their best to bring him

The Wound Dresser

to — three long hours were spent, a strong smelling bottle held under his nostrils, with other means, three hours. Mother, how contemptible all the usual little worldly prides and vanities, and striving after appearances, seems in the midst of such scenes as these — such tragedies of soul and body. To see such things and not be able to help them is awful — I feel almost ashamed of being so well and whole.

Dear mother, I have not heard from George himself; but I got a letter from Fred McReady, a young Brooklyn man in 51st — he is intimate with George, said he was well and hearty. I got the letter about five days ago. I wrote to George four days since, directed to Winchester, Kentucky. I got a letter from a friend in Nashville, Tenn., yesterday — he told me the 9th Army Corps was ordered to move to Murfreesboro, Tenn. I don't know whether this is so or not. I send papers to George almost every day. So far I think it was fortunate the 51st was moved West, and I hope it will continue so. Mother, it is all a lottery, this war; no one knows what will come up next.

Mother, I received Jeff's letter of May 9th — it was welcome, as all Jeff's letters are, and all others from home. Jeff says you do not hear from me at home but seldom. Mother, I write once a week to you regular; but I will write soon to Jeff a good long letter — I have wanted to for some time, but have been much occupied. Dear brother, I wish you to say to Probasco and

Letters of 1862-3

all the other young men on the Works, I send them my love and best thanks — never anything came more acceptable than the little fund they forwarded me the last week through Mr. Lane. Our wounded from Hooker's battles are worse wounded and more of them than any battle of the war, and indeed any, I may say, of modern times — besides, the weather has been very hot here, very bad for new wounds. Yet as Jeff writes so downhearted I must tell him the Rebellion has lost worse and more than we have. The more I find out about it, the more I think they, the Confederates, have received an irreparable harm and loss in Virginia — I should not be surprised to see them (either voluntarily or by force) leaving Virginia before many weeks; I don't see how on earth they can stay there. I think Hooker is already reaching after them again — I myself do not give up Hooker yet. Dear mother, I should like to hear from Han, poor Han. I send my best love to sister Mat and all. Good-bye, dearest mother. WALT.

XI

Washington, Tuesday forenoon, May 19, 1863.
DEAREST MOTHER — . . . . I sent George a letter yesterday — have not got any letter myself from Georgy, but have sent him quite a good many and papers. Mother, what a tramp the 51st has had — they only need now to go to

The Wound Dresser

California, and they will finish the job complete. O mother, how welcome the shirts were — I was putting off and putting off, to get some new ones. I could not find any one to do them as I want them, and it would have cost such a price — and so my old ones had got to be. When they came back from the wash I had to laugh; they were a lot of rags, held together with starch. I have a very nice old black aunty for a washwoman, but she bears down pretty hard, I guess, when she irons them, and they showed something like the poor old city of Fredericksburg does, since Burnside bombarded it. Well, mother, when the bundle came, I was so glad — and the coats too, worn as they are, they come in very handy — and the cake, dear mother, I am almost like the boy that put it under his pillow and woke up in the night and eat some. I carried a good chunk to a young man wounded I think a good deal of, and it did him so much good — it is dry, but all the better, as he eat it with tea and it relished. I eat a piece with him, and drinked some tea out of his cup, as I sat by the side of his cot. Mother, I have neglected, I think, what I ought to have told you two or three weeks ago, that is that I have discarded my old clothes — somewhat because they were too thick, and more still because they were worse gone in than any I have ever yet wore, I think, in my life, especially the trowsers. Wearing my big boots had caused the inside of the legs just above the knee to wear two beautiful round holes right through cloth and partly through the lin-

Letters of 1862-3

ing, producing a novel effect, which was not necessary, as I produce a sufficient sensation without — then they were desperately faded. I have a nice plain suit of a dark wine color; looks very well, and feels good — single breasted sack coat with breast pockets, etc., and vest and pants same as what I always wear (pants pretty full), so upon the whole all looks unusually good for me. My hat is very good yet, boots ditto; have a new necktie, nice shirts — you can imagine I cut quite a swell. I have not trimmed my beard since I left home, but it is not grown much longer, only perhaps a little bushier. I keep about as stout as ever, and the past fiye or six days I have felt wonderful well, indeed never did I feel better. About ten or twelve days ago, we had a short spell of very warm weather here, but for about six days now it has been delightful, just warm enough. I generally go to the hospitals from 12 to 4 — and then again from 6 to 9; some days I only go in the middle of the day or evening, not both — and then when I feel somewhat opprest, I skip over a day, or make perhaps a light call only, as I have several cautions from the doctors, who tell me that one must beware of continuing too steady and long in the air and influences of the hospitals. I find the caution a wise one.

Mother, you or Jeff must write me what Andrew does about going to North Carolina. I should think it might have a beneficial effect upon his throat. I wrote Jeff quite a long letter

The Wound Dresser

Sunday. Jeff must write to me whenever he can, I like dearly to have them — and whenever you feel like it you too, dear mother. Tell Sis her uncle Walt will come back one of these days from the sick soldiers and take her out on Fort Greene again. Mother, I received a letter yesterday from John Elliot's father, in Bedford co., Pennsylvania (the young man I told you about, who died under the operation). It was very sad; it was the first he knew about it. I don't know whether I told you of Dennis Barrett, pneumonia three weeks since, had got well enough to be sent home. Dearest mother, I hope you will take things as easy as possible and try to keep a good heart. Matty, my dear sister, I have to inform you that I was treated to a splendid dish of ice-cream Sunday night; I wished you was with me to have another. I send you my love, dear sister. Mother, I hope by all means it will be possible to keep the money whole to get some ranch next spring, if not before; I mean to come home and build it. Good-bye for the present, dear mother. WALT.

XII

Washington, Tuesday forenoon, May 26, 1863.
DEAREST MOTHER — I got a long letter from George, dated near Lancaster, Kentucky, May 15th; he seems to be well and in good spirits — says he gets some letters from me and papers too. At the time he wrote the 51st was doing

Letters of 1862-3

provost duty at Lancaster, but would not probably remain so very long — seem to be moving towards southeast Kentucky — had a good camp, and good times generally. Le Gendre is colonel — Gen. Ferrero has left the service — Col. Potter (now brig.-gen.) is in Cincinnati — Capt. Sims, etc., are all well. George describes Kentucky as a very fine country — says the people are about half and half, Secesh and Union. This is the longest letter I have yet received from George. Did he write you one about the same time? Mother, I have not rec'd any word from home in over a week — the last letter I had from Mr. Lane was about twelve days ago, sending me $10 for the soldiers (five from Mr. Kirkwood and five from Mr. Conklin Brush). Mother dear, I should like to hear from Martha; I wish Jeff would write me about it. Has Andrew gone? and how is your wrist and arm, mother? We had some very hot weather here — I don't know what I should have done without the thin grey coat you sent — you don't know how good it does, and looks too; I wore it three days, and carried a fan and an umbrella (quite a Japanee) — most everybody here carries an umbrella, on account of the sun. Yesterday and to-day however have been quite cool, east wind. Mother, the shirts were a real godsend, they do first rate; I like the fancy marseilles collar and wristbands. Mother, how are you getting along — I suppose just the same as ever. I suppose Jess and Ed are just the same as ever. When

The Wound Dresser

you write, you tell me all about everything, and the Browns, and the neighborhood generally. Mother, is George's trunk home and of no use there? I wish I had it here, as I must have a trunk — but do not wish you to send until I send you word. I suppose my letter never appeared in the *Eagle*; well, I shall send them no more, as I think likely they hate to put in anything which may celebrate me a little, even though it is just the thing they want for their paper and readers. They altered the other letter on that account, very meanly. I shall probably have letters in the N. Y. *Times* and perhaps other papers in about a week. Mother, I have been pretty active in hospitals for the past two weeks, somewhere every day or night. I have written you so much about cases, etc., I will not write you any more on that subject this time. O the sad, sad things I see — the noble young men with legs and arms taken off — the deaths — the sick weakness, sicker than death, that some endure, after amputations (there is a great difference, some make little of it, others lie after it for days, just flickering alive, and O so deathly weak and sick). I go this afternoon to Campbell hospital, out a couple of miles.

Mother, I should like to have Jeff send me 20 of the large-sized portraits and as many of the standing figure; do them up flat. I think every day about Martha. Mother, have you heard any further about Han? Good-bye for the present, dearest mother. WALT.

Letters of 1862-3

XIII

Washington, Tuesday morning, June 9, 1863.
DEAREST MOTHER — Jeff's letter came yesterday and was very welcome, as I wanted to hear about you all. I wrote to George yesterday and sent Jeff's letter enclosed. It looks from some accounts as though the 9th Army Corps might be going down into East Tennessee (Cumberland Gap, or perhaps bound for Knoxville). It is an important region, and has many Southern Unionists. The staunchest Union man I have ever met is a young Southerner in the 2nd Tennessee (Union reg't) — he was ten months in Southern prisons; came up from Richmond paroled about ten weeks ago, and has been in hospital here sick until lately. He suffered everything but death — he is [the] one they hung up by the heels, head downwards — and indeed worse than death, but stuck to his convictions like a hero — John Barker, a real manly fellow; I saw much of him and heard much of that country that can be relied on. He is now gone home to his reg't.

Mother, I am feeling very well these days — my head that was stopt up so and hard of hearing seems to be all right; I only hope you have had similar good fortune with your rheumatism, and that it will continue so. I wish I could come in for a couple of days and see you; if I should succeed in getting a transportation ticket that would take me to New York and back I should be tempted to come home for two or three days, as I

The Wound Dresser

want some MSS. and books, and the trunk, etc. — but I will see. Mother, your letter week before last was very good — whenever you feel like it you write me, dear mother, and tell me everything about the neighborhood and all the items of our family.

And sister Mat, how is she getting along — I believe I will have to write a letter especially to her and Sis one of these times.

It is awful dry weather here, no rain of any consequence for five or six weeks. We have strawberries good and plenty, 15 cents a quart, with the hulls on — I go down to market sometimes of a morning and buy two or three quarts, for the folks I take my meals with. Mother, do you know I have not paid, as you may say, a cent of board since I have been in Washington, that is for meals — four or five times I have made a rush to leave the folks and find a moderate-priced boarding-house, but every time they have made such a time about it that I have kept on. It is Mr. and Mrs. O'Connor (he is the author of "Harrington"); he has a $1600 office in the Treasury, and she is a first-rate woman, a Massachusetts girl. They keep house in a moderate way; they have one little girl (lost a fine boy about a year ago); they have two rooms in the same house where I hire my rooms, and I take breakfast (half-past 8) and dinner (half-past 4) with them, as they will have it so. That's the way it has gone on now over five months, and as I say, they won't listen to my leaving — but I shall do so, I think. I can

Letters of 1862-3

never forget the kindness and real friendship, and it appears as though they would continue just the same, if it were for all our lives. But I have insisted on going to market (it is pleasant in the cool of the morning) and getting the things at my own expense, two or three times a week lately. I pay for the room I occupy now $7 a month — the landlord is a mixture of booby, miser, and hog; his name is G——; the landlady is a good woman, Washington raised — they are quite rich; he is Irish of the worst kind — has had a good office for ten years until Lincoln came in. They have bought another house, smaller, to live in, and are going to move (were to have moved 1st of June). They had an auction of the house we live in yesterday, but nobody came to buy, so it was ridiculous — we had a red flag out, and a nigger walked up and down ringing a big bell, which is the fashion here for auctions.

Well, mother, the war still goes on, and everything as much in a fog as ever — and the battles as bloody, and the wounded and sick getting worse and plentier all the time. I see a letter in the *Tribune* from Lexington, Ky., June 5th, headed "The 9th Army Corps departing for Vicksburg" — but I cannot exactly make it out on reading the letter carefully — I don't see anything in the letter about the 9th Corps moving from Vicksburg; at any rate I think the 2nd division is more likely to be needed in Kentucky (or as I said, in Eastern Tennessee), as the Secesh are expected to make trouble there. But one can hardly tell — the

The Wound Dresser

only thing is to resign oneself to events as they occur; it is a sad and dreary time, for so many thousands of parents and relatives, not knowing what will occur next. Mother, I told you, I think last week, that I had wrote to Han, and enclosed George's last letter to me — I wrote a week ago last Sunday — I wonder if she got the letter. About the pictures, I should like Jeff to send them, as soon as convenient — might send 20 of the big head, 10 or 12 of the standing figure, and 3 of the carte visite.

I am writing this in Major Hapgood's office — it is bright and pleasant, only the dust here in Washington is a great nuisance. Mother, your shirts do first rate — I am wearing them; the one I have on to-day suits me better than any I have ever yet had. I have not worn the thin coat the last week or so, as it has not been very hot lately. Mother, I think something of commencing a series of lectures and reading, etc., through different cities of the North, to supply myself with funds for my hospital and soldiers' visits, as I do not like to be beholden to the medium of others. I need a pretty large supply of money, etc., to do the good I would like to, and the work grows upon me, and fascinates me — it is the most affecting thing you ever see, the lots of poor sick and wounded young men that depend so much, in one word or another, upon my petting or soothing or feeding, sitting by them and feeding them their dinner or supper — some are quite helpless, some wounded in both arms — or giving

Letters of 1862-3

some trifle (for a novelty or a change, it is n't for the value of it), or stopping a little while with them. Nobody will do but me — so, mother, I feel as though I would like to inaugurate a plan by which I could raise means on my own hook, and perhaps quite plenty too. Best love to you, dearest mother, and to sister Mat, and Jeff. WALT.

XIV

Washington, Monday morning, June 22, 1863.
DEAR MOTHER — Jeff's letter came informing me of the birth of the little girl,[1] and that Matty was feeling pretty well, so far. I hope it will continue. Dear sister, I should much like to come home and see you and the little one; I am sure from Jeff's description it is a noble babe — and as to its being a girl, it is all the better. (I am not sure but the Whitman breed gives better women than men.)

Well, mother, we are generally anticipating a lively time here, or in the neighborhood, as it is probable Lee is feeling about to strike a blow on Washington, or perhaps right into it — and as Lee is no fool, it is perhaps possible he may give us a good shake. He is not very far off — yesterday was a fight to the southwest of here all day; we heard the cannons nearly all day. The wounded are arriving in small squads every day, mostly cavalry, a great many Ohio men; they

[1] Jessie Louisa Whitman.

The Wound Dresser

send off to-day from the Washington hospitals a great many to New York, Philadelphia, etc., all who are able, to make room, which looks ominous — indeed, it is pretty certain that there is to be some severe fighting, may-be a great battle again, the pending week. I am getting so callous that it hardly arouses me at all. I fancy I should take it very quietly if I found myself in the midst of a desperate conflict here in Washington.

Mother, I have nothing particular to write about — I see and hear nothing but new and old cases of my poor suffering boys in hospitals, and I dare say you have had enough of such things. I have not missed a day at hospital, I think, for more than three weeks — I get more and more wound round. Poor young men — there are some cases that would literally sink and give up if I did not pass a portion of the time with them. I have quite made up my mind about the lecturing, etc., project — I have no doubt it will succeed well enough the way I shall put it in operation. You know, mother, it is to raise funds to enable me to continue my hospital ministrations, on a more free-handed scale. As to the Sanitary commissions and the like, I am sick of them all, and would not accept any of their berths. You ought to see the way the men, as they lay helpless in bed, turn away their faces from the sight of those agents, chaplains, etc. (hirelings, as Elias Hicks would call them — they seem to me always a set of foxes and wolves). They get well paid, and

Letters of 1862–3

are always incompetent and disagreeable; as I told you before, the only good fellows I have met are the Christian commissioners — they go everywhere and receive no pay.

Dear, dear mother, I want much to see you, and dear Matty too; I send you both my best love, and Jeff too. The pictures came — I have not heard from George nor Han. I write a day earlier than usual. WALT.

We here think Vicksburg is ours. The probability is that it has capitulated — and there has been no general assault — can't tell yet whether the 51st went there. We are having very fine weather here to-day — rained last night.

XV

Washington, June 30th, 1863. DEAREST MOTHER — Your letter, with Han's, I have sent to George, though whether it will find him or not I cannot tell, as I think the 51st must be away down at Vicksburg. I have not had a word from George yet. Mother, I have had quite an attack of sore throat and distress in my head for some days past, up to last night, but to-day I feel nearly all right again. I have been about the city same as usual nearly — to the hospitals, etc., I mean. I am told that I hover too much over the beds of the hospitals, with fever and putrid wounds, etc. One soldier brought here about fifteen days ago, very low with typhoid fever, Livingston

The Wound Dresser

Brooks, Co. B., 17th Penn. Cavalry, I have particularly stuck to, as I found him to be in what appeared to be a dying condition, from negligence and a horrible journey of about forty miles, bad roads and fast driving; and then after he got here, as he is a simple country boy, very shy and silent, and made no complaint, they neglected him. I found him something like I found John Holmes last winter. I called the doctor's attention to him, shook up the nurses, had him bathed in spirits, gave him lumps of ice, and ice to his head; he had a fearful bursting pain in his head, and his body was like fire. He was very quiet, a very sensible boy, old fashioned; he did not want to die, and I had to lie to him without stint, for he thought I knew everything, and I always put in of course that what I told him was exactly the truth, and that if he got really dangerous I would tell him and not conceal it. The rule is to remove bad fever patients out from the main wards to a tent by themselves, and the doctor told me he would have to be removed. I broke it gently to him, but the poor boy got it immediately in his head that he was marked with death, and was to be removed on that account. It had a great effect upon him, and although I told the truth this time it did not have as good a result as my former fibs. I persuaded the doctor to let him remain. For three days he lay just about an even chance, go or stay, with a little leaning toward the first. But, mother, to make a long story short, he is now out of any immediate danger.

Letters of 1862-3

He has been perfectly rational throughout — begins to taste a little food (for a week he ate nothing; I had to compel him to take a quarter of an orange now and then), and I will say, whether anyone calls it pride or not, that if he *does* get up and around again it's me that saved his life. Mother, as I have said in former letters, you can have no idea how these sick and dying youngsters cling to a fellow, and how fascinating it is, with all its hospital surroundings of sadness and scenes of repulsion and death. In this same hospital, Armory-square, where this cavalry boy is, I have about fifteen or twenty particular cases I see much to — some of them as much as him. There are two from East Brooklyn: George Monk, Co. A, 78th N. Y., and Stephen Redgate (his mother is a widow in East Brooklyn — I have written to her). Both are pretty badly wounded — both are youngsters under 19. O mother, it seems to to me as I go through these rows of cots as if it was too bad to accept these *children*, to subject them to such premature experiences. I devote myself much to Armory-square hospital because it contains by far the worst cases, most repulsive wounds, has the most suffering and most need of consolation. I go every day without fail, and often at night — sometimes stay very late. No one interferes with me, guards, nurses, doctors, nor anyone. I am let to take my own course.

Well, mother, I suppose you folks think we are in a somewhat dubious position here in Washington, with Lee in strong force almost between

The Wound Dresser

us and you Northerners. Well, it does look ticklish; if the Rebs cut the connection then there will be fun. The Reb cavalry come quite near us, dash in and steal wagon trains, etc.; it would be funny if they should come some night to the President's country house (Soldiers' home), where he goes out to sleep every night; it is in the same direction as their saucy raid last Sunday. Mr. Lincoln passes here (14th st.) every evening on his way out. I noticed him last evening about half-past 6 — he was in his barouche, two horses, guarded by about thirty cavalry. The barouche comes first under a slow trot, driven by one man in the box, no servant or footman beside; the cavalry all follow closely after with a lieutenant at their head. I had a good view of the President last evening. He looks more careworn even than usual, his face with deep cut lines, seams, and his *complexion gray* through very dark skin — a curious looking man, very sad. I said to a lady who was looking with me, "Who can see that man without losing all wish to be sharp upon him personally?" The lady assented, although she is almost vindictive on the course of the administration (thinks it wants nerve, etc. — the usual complaint). The equipage is rather shabby, horses indeed almost what my friends the Broadway drivers would call *old plugs*. The President dresses in plain black clothes, cylinder hat — he was alone yesterday. As he came up, he first drove over to the house of the Sec. of War, on K st., about 300 feet from

Letters of 1862-3

here; sat in his carriage while Stanton came out and had a 15 minutes interview with him (I can see from my window), and then wheeled around the corner and up Fourteenth st., the cavalry after him. I really think it would be safer for him just now to stop at the White House, but I expect he is too proud to abandon the former custom. Then about an hour after we had a large cavalry regiment pass, with blankets, arms, etc., on the war march over the same track. The regt. was very full, over a thousand — indeed thirteen or fourteen hundred. It was an old regt., veterans, *old fighters,* young as they were. They were preceded by a fine mounted band of sixteen (about ten bugles, the rest cymbals and drums). I tell you, mother, it made everything ring — made my heart leap. They played with a will. Then the accompaniment: the sabers rattled on a thousand men's sides — they had pistols, their heels were spurred — handsome American young men (I make no acc't of any other); rude uniforms, well worn, but good cattle, prancing — all good riders, full of the devil; nobody shaved, very sunburnt. The regimental officers (splendidly mounted, but just as roughly dressed as the men) came immediately after the band, then company after company, with each its officers at its head — the tramps of so many horses (there is a good hard turnpike) — then a long train of men with led horses, mounted negroes, and a long, long string of baggage wagons, each with four horses, and then a strong

The Wound Dresser

rear guard. I tell you it had the look of *real war* — noble looking fellows; a man feels so proud on a good horse, and armed. They are off toward the region of Lee's (supposed) rendezvous, toward Susquehannah, for the great anticipated battle. Alas! how many of these healthy, handsome, rollicking young men will lie cold in death before the apples ripen in the orchard. Mother, it is curious and stirring here in some respects. Smaller or larger bodies of troops are moving continually — many just-well men are turned out of the hospitals. I am where I see a good deal of them. There are getting to be *many black troops*. There is one very good regt. here black as tar; they go around, have the regular uniform — they submit to no nonsense. Others are constantly forming. It is getting to be a common sight. [*The rest of the letter is lost.* — ED.]

XVI

Washington, July 10, 1863. DEAR MOTHER — I suppose you rec'd a letter from me last Wednesday, as I sent you one Tuesday (7th). Dear mother, I was glad enough to hear from George, by that letter from Snyder's Bluffs, June 28th. I had felt a little fear on acc't of some of those storming parties Grant sent against Vicksburg the middle of June and up to the 20th — but this letter dispels all anxiety. I have written to George many times, but it seems he has not got them. Mother, I shall write immediately to him again. I think he will get the letter I sent last Sunday, as I directed it to Vicksburg — I told him all the news from home. Mother, I shall write to Han and enclose George's letter. I am real glad to hear from Mat and the little one, all so favorable. We are having pleasant weather here still. I go to Campbell hospital this afternoon — I still keep going, mother. The wounded are doing rather badly; I am sorry to say there are frequent deaths — the weather, I suppose, which has been peculiarly bad for wounds, so wet and warm (though not disagreeable outdoors). Mother, you must write as often as you can, and Jeff too — you must not get worried about the ups and downs of the war; I don't know any course but to resign oneself to events — if one can only bring one's mind to it. Good-bye once more, for the present, dearest mother, Mat, and the dear little ones. WALT.

Mother, do you ever hear from Mary?[1]

XVII

Washington, Wednesday forenoon, July 15, 1863.
DEAR MOTHER — So the mob has risen at last in New York — I have been expecting it, but as the day for the draft had arrived and everything was so quiet, I supposed all might go on smoothly; but it seems the passions of the

[1] His sister, Mary Elizabeth Whitman (Mrs. Van Nostrand) born 1821 now (1897) residing in Sag Harbor, L. I.

The Wound Dresser

people were only sleeping, and have burst forth with terrible fury, and they have destroyed life and property, the enrolment buildings, etc., as we hear. The accounts we get are a good deal in a muddle, but it seems bad enough. The feeling here is savage and hot as fire against New York (the mob — "Copperhead mob" the papers here call it), and I hear nothing in all directions but threats of ordering up the gunboats, cannonading the city, shooting down the mob, hanging them in a body, etc., etc. Meantime I remain silent, partly amused, partly scornful, or occasionally put a dry remark, which only adds fuel to the flame. I do not feel it in my heart to abuse the poor people, or call for a rope or bullets for them, but that is all the talk here, even in the hospitals. The acc'ts from N. Y. this morning are that the Gov't has ordered the draft to be suspended there — I hope it is true, for I find that the deeper they go in with the draft, the more trouble it is likely to make. I have changed my opinion and feelings on the subject — we are in the midst of strange and terrible times — one is pulled a dozen different ways in his mind, and hardly knows what to think or do. Mother, I have not much fear that the troubles in New York will affect any of our family, still I feel somewhat uneasy about Jeff, if any one, as he is more around. I have had it much on my mind what could be done, if it should so happen that Jeff should be drafted — of course he could not go without its being the

Letters of 1862-3

downfall almost of our whole family, as you may say, Mat and his young ones, and sad blow to you too, mother, and to all. I did n't see any other way than to try to raise the $300, mostly by borrowing if possible of Mr. Lane. Mother, I have no doubt I shall make a few hundred dollars by the lectures I shall certainly commence soon (for my hospital missionary purposes and my own, for that purpose), and I could lend that am't to Jeff to pay it back. May-be the draft will not come off after all; I should say it was very doubtful if they can carry it out in N. Y. and Brooklyn — and besides, it is only one chance out of several, to be drawn if it does. I don't wonder dear brother Jeff feels the effect it would have on domestic affairs; I think it is right to feel so, full as strongly as a man can. I do hope all will go well and without such an additional trouble falling upon us, but as it can be met with money, I hope Jeff and Mat and all of you, dear mother, will not worry any more about it. I wrote to Jeff a few lines last Sunday, I suppose he got. Mother, I don't know whether you have had a kind of gloomy week the past week, but somehow I feel as if you all had; but I hope it has passed over. How is dear sister Mat, and how is Miss Manna-hatta, and little Black Head? I sometimes feel as if I *must* come home and see you all — I want to very much.

My hospital life still continues the same — I was in Armory all day yesterday — and day

The Wound Dresser

and night before. They have the men wounded in the railroad accident at Laurel station (bet. here and Baltimore), about 30 soldiers, some of them horribly injured at 3 o'clock A.M. last Saturday by collision — poor, poor, poor men. I go again this afternoon and night — I see so much of butcher sights, so much sickness and suffering, I must get away a while, I believe, for self-preservation. I have felt quite well though the past week — we have had rain continually. Mother, I have not heard from George since, have you? I shall write Han to-day and send George's letter — if you or Jeff has not written this week, I hope Jeff will write on receiving this. Good-bye for present, dearest mother, and Jeff, and Mat. WALT.

Mother, the army is to be paid off two months more, right away. Of course George will get two months more pay. Dear mother, I hope you will keep untouched and put in bank every cent you can. I want us to have a ranch somewhere by or before next spring.

XVIII

Washington, Aug. 11, 1863. DEAR MOTHER — I sent Jeff a letter on Sunday — I suppose he got it at the office. I feel so anxious to hear from George; one cannot help feeling uneasy, although these days sometimes it cannot help

Letters of 1862-3

being long intervals without one's hearing from friends in the army. O I do hope we shall hear soon, and that it is all right with him. It seems as if the 9th Corps had returned to Vicksburg, and some acc'ts say that part of the Corps had started to come up the river again — toward Kentucky, I suppose. I have sent George two letters within a week past, hoping they might have the luck to get to him, but hardly expect it either.

Mother, I feel very sorry to hear Andrew is so troubled in his throat yet. I know it must make you feel very unhappy. Jeff wrote me a good deal about it, and seems to feel very bad about Andrew's being unwell; but I hope it will go over, and that a little time will make him recover — I think about it every day.

Mother, it has been the hottest weather here that I ever experienced, and still continues so. Yesterday and last night was the hottest. Still, I slept sound, have good ventilation through my room, little as it is (I still hire the same room in L street). I was quite wet with sweat this morning when I woke up, a thing I never remember to have happened to me before, for I was not disturbed in my sleep and did not wake up once all night. Mother, I believe I did not tell you that on the 1st of June (or a while before) the O'Connors, the friends I took my meals with so long, moved to other apartments for more room and pleasanter — not far off though, I am there every day almost, a little — so for nearly two

The Wound Dresser

months and a half I have been in the habit of getting my own breakfast in my room and my dinner at a restaurant. I have a little spirit lamp, and always have a capital cup of tea, and some bread, and perhaps some preserved fruit; for dinner I get a good plate of meat and plenty of potatoes, good and plenty for 25 or 30 cents. I hardly ever take any thing more than these two meals, both of them are pretty hearty — eat dinner about 3 — my appetite is plenty good enough, and I am about as fleshy as I was in Brooklyn. Mother, I feel better the last ten days, and at present, than I did the preceding six or eight weeks. There was nothing particular the matter with me, but I suppose a different climate and being so continually in the hospitals — but as I say, I feel better, more strength, and better in my head, etc. About the wound in my hand and the inflammation, etc., it has thoroughly healed, and I have not worn anything on my hand, nor had any dressing for the last five days. Mother, I hope you get along with the heat, for I see it is as bad or worse in New York and Brooklyn — I am afraid you suffer from it; it must be distressing to you. Dear mother, do let things go, and just sit still and fan yourself. I think about you these hot days. I fancy I see you down there in the basement. I suppose you have your coffee for breakfast; I have not had three cups of coffee in six months — tea altogether (I must come home and have some coffee for breakfast with you).

Letters of 1862-3

Mother, I wrote to you about Erastus Haskell, Co. K, 141st, N. Y. — his father, poor old man, come on here to see him and found him dead three days. He had the body embalmed and took home. They are poor folks but very respectable. I was at the hospital yesterday as usual — I never miss a day. I go by my feelings — if I should feel that it would be better for me to lay by for a while, I should do so, but not while I feel so well as I do the past week, for all the hot weather; and while the chance lasts I would improve it, for by and by the night cometh when no man can work (ain't I getting pious!). I got a letter from Probasco yesterday; he sent $4 for my sick and wounded — I wish Jeff to tell him that it came right, and give him the men's thanks and my love.

Mother, have you heard anything from Han? And about Mary's Fanny — I hope you will write me soon and tell me everything, tell me exactly as things are, but I know you will — I want to hear family affairs before anything else. I am so glad to hear Mat is good and hearty — you must write me about Hat and little Black Head too. Mother, how is Eddy getting along? and Jess, is he about the same? I suppose Will Brown is home all right; tell him I spoke about him, and the Browns too. Dearest mother, I send you my love, and to Jeff too — must write when you can. WALT.

The Wound Dresser

XIX

Washington, Aug. 18, 1863. DEAR MOTHER — I was mighty glad to get George's letter, I can tell you — you have not heard since, I suppose. They must be now back again in Kentucky, or that way, as I see [by] a letter from Cairo (up the Mississippi river) that boats had stopt there with the 9th Corps on from Vicksburg, going up towards Cincinnati — I think the letter was dated Aug. 10. I have no doubt they are back again up that way somewhere. I wrote to George four or five days ago — I directed it Ohio, Mississippi, or elsewhere. Mother, I was very glad indeed to get your letter — I am so sorry Andrew does not get any better; it is very distressing about losing the voice; he must not be so much alarmed, as that continues some times years and the health otherwise good.
. . . . Mother, I wrote to Han about five days ago; told her we had heard from George, and all the news — I must write to Mary too, without fail — I should like to hear from them all, and from Fanny. There has been a young man here in hospital, from Farmingdale; he was wounded; his name is Hendrickson; he has gone home on a furlough; he knows the Van Nostrands very well — I told him to go and see Aunt Fanny. I was glad you gave Emma Price my direction here; I should [like] to hear from Mrs. Price and her girls first rate, I think a great deal about them — and mother, I wish you to tell any of them so; they always used me first rate, and

Letters of 1862-3

always stuck up for me — if I knew their street and number I should write.

It has been awful hot here now for twenty-one days; ain't that a spell of weather? The first two weeks I got along better than I would have thought, but the last week I have felt it more, have felt it in my head a little — I no more stir without my umbrella, in the day time, than I would without my boots. I am afraid of the sun affecting my head and move pretty cautious. Mother, I think every day, I wonder if the hot weather is affecting mother much; I suppose it must a good deal, but I hope it cannot last much longer. Mother, I had a letter in the N. Y. *Times* of last Sunday — did you see it? I wonder if George can't get a furlough and come home for a while; that furlough he had was only a flea-bite. If he could it would be no more than right, for no man in the country has done his duty more faithful, and without complaining of anything or asking for anything, than George. I suppose they will fill up the 51st with conscripts, as that seems the order of the day — a good many are arriving here, from the North, and passing through to join Meade's army. We are expecting to hear of more rows in New York about the draft; it commences there right away I see — this time it will be no such doings as a month or five weeks ago; the Gov't here is forwarding a large force of regulars to New York to be ready for anything that may happen — there will be no blank cartridges this time. Well, I

The Wound Dresser

thought when I first heard of the riot in N. Y. I had some feeling for them, but soon as I found what it really was, I felt it was the devil's own work all through. I guess the strong arm will be exhibited this time up to the shoulder. Mother, I want to see you and all very much. As I wish to be here at the opening of Congress, and during the winter, I have an idea I will try to come home for a month, but I don't know when — I want to see the young ones and Mat and Jeff and everybody. Well, mother, I should like to know all the domestic affairs at home; don't you have the usual things eating, etc.? Why, mother, I should think you would eat nearly all your meals with Mat — I know you must when they have anything good (and I know Mat will have good things if she has got a cent left). Mother, don't you miss *Walt* loafing around, and carting himself off to New York toward the latter part of every afternoon? How do you and the Browns get along? — that hell hole over the way, what a nuisance it must be nights, and I generally have a very good sleep. Mother, I suppose you sleep in the back room yet — I suppose the new houses next door are occupied. How I should like to take a walk on old Fort Greene — tell Mannahatta her Uncle Walt will be home yet, from the sick soldiers, and have a good walk all around, if she behaves to her grandmother and don't cut up. Mother, I am scribbling this hastily in Major Hapgood's office; it is not so hot to-day, quite endurable. I send you my love, dear

Letters of 1862-3

mother, and to all, and wish Jeff and you to write as often as you can. WALT.

XX

Washington, Aug. 25, 1863. DEAR MOTHER— The letter from George, and your lines, and a few from Jeff came yesterday, and I was glad indeed to be certain that George had got back to Kentucky safe and well — while so many fall that we know, or, what is about as bad, get sick or hurt in the fight, and lay in hospital, it seems almost a miracle that George should have gone through so much, South and North and East and West, and been in so many hard-fought battles, and thousands of miles of weary and exhausting marches, and yet have stood it so, and be yet alive and in good health and spirits. O mother, what would we [have] done if it had been otherwise — if he had met the fate of so many we know — if he had been killed or badly hurt in some of those battles? I get thinking about it sometimes, and it works upon me so I have to stop and turn my mind on something else. Mother, I feel bad enough about Andrew, and I know it must be so with you too — one don't know what to do; if we had money he would be welcome to it, if it would do any good. If George's money comes from Kentucky this last time, and you think some of it would do Andrew any real good, I advise you to take some and give him — I think it would be proper and George would

The Wound Dresser

approve of it. I believe there is not much but trouble in this world, and if one has n't any for himself he has it made up by having it brought close to him through others, and that is sometimes worse than to have it touch one's self. Mother, you must not let Andrew's case and the poor condition of his household comforts, etc., work upon you, for I fear you will — but, mother, it's no use to worry about such things. I have seen so much horrors that befall men (so bad and such suffering and mutilations, etc., that the poor men can defy their fate to do anything more or any harder misfortune or worse a-going) that I sometimes think I have grown callous — but no, I don't think it is that, but nothing of ordinary misfortune seems as it used to, and death itself has lost all its terrors — I have seen so many cases in which it was so welcome and such a relief.

Mother, you must just resign yourself to things that occur — but I hardly think it is necessary to give you any charge about it, for I think you have done so for many years, and stood it all with good courage.

We have a second attack of hot weather — Sunday was the most burning day I ever yet saw. It is very dry and dusty here, but to-day we are having a middling good breeze — I feel pretty well, and whenever the weather for a day or so is passably cool I feel really first rate, so I anticipate the cooler season with pleasure. Mother, I believe I wrote to you I had a letter in N. Y. *Times*, Sunday, 16th — I shall try to write others and more frequently. The three *Eagles* came safe; I was glad to get them — I sent them and another paper to George. Mother, none of you ever mention whether you get my letters, but I suppose they come safe — it is not impossible I may miss some week, but I have not missed a single one for months past. I wish I could send you something worth while, and I wish I could send something for Andrew — mother, write me exactly how it is with him. . . . . Mother, I have some idea Han is getting some better; it is only my idea somehow — I hope it is so from the bottom of my heart. Did you hear from Mary's Fanny since? And how are Mat's girls? So, Mannahatta, you tear Uncle George's letters, do you? You must n't do so, little girl, nor Uncle Walt's either; but when you get to be a big girl you must have them all nice, and read them, for Grandmother will perhaps leave them to you in her will, if you behave like a lady. Matty, my dear sister, how are you getting along? I really want to see you bad, and the baby too — well, may-be we shall all come together and have some good times yet. Jeff, I hope by next week this time we shall be in possession of Charleston — some papers say Burnside is moving for Knoxville, but it is doubtful — I think the 9th Corps might take a rest awhile, anyhow. Good-bye, mother. WALT.

The Wound Dresser

XXI

Washington, Sept. 1, 1863. DEAR MOTHER — I have been thinking to-day and all yesterday about the draft in Brooklyn, and whether Jeff would be drafted; you must some of you write me just as soon as you get this — I want to know; I feel anxious enough I can tell you — and besides, it seems a good while since I have received any letters from home. Of course it is impossible for Jeff to go, in case it should turn out he was drafted — the way our family is all situated now, it would be madness. If the Common Council raise the money to exempt men with families dependent on them, I think Jeff ought to have no scruples in taking advantage of it, as I think he is in duty bound — but we will see what course to take, when we know the result, etc.; write about it right away.

The *Eagles* came; this is the second time; I am glad to get them — Jeff, wait till you get four or five, and then send them with a two-cent stamp. I have not had any letter from George. Mother, have you heard anything? did the money come? Dear mother, how are you nowadays? I do hope you feel well and in good spirits — I think about you every day of my life out here. Sometimes I see women in the hospitals, mothers come to see their sons, and occasionally one that makes me think of my dear mother — one did very much, a lady about 60, from Pennsylvania, come to see her son, a captain, very badly

Letters of 1862-3

wounded and his wound gangrened, and they after a while removed him to a tent by himself. Another son of hers, a young man, came with her to see his brother. She was a pretty full-sized lady, with spectacles; she dressed in black — looked real Velsory.[1] I got very well acquainted with her; she had a real Long Island old-fashioned way — but I had to avoid the poor captain, as it was that time that my hand was cut in the artery, and I was liable to gangrene myself — but she and the two sons have gone home now, but I doubt whether the wounded one is alive, as he was very low. Mother, I want to hear about Andrew too, whether he went to Rockland lake. You have no idea how many soldiers there are who have lost their voices, and have to speak in whispers — there are a great many, I meet some almost every day; as far as that alone is concerned, Andrew must not be discouraged, as the general health may be good as common irrespective of that. I do hope Andrew will get along better than he thinks for — it is bad enough for a poor man to be out of health even partially, but he must try to look on the bright side. Mother, have you heard anything from Han since, or from Mary's folks? I got a letter from Mrs. Price last week; if you see Emma tell her I was pleased to get it, and shall answer it very soon. Mother, I have sent another letter to the N. Y. *Times* — it may appear, if not to-day, within a few days. I am feeling excellent well these

[1] Mrs. Whitman's maiden name was Louisa Van Velsor.

The Wound Dresser

days, it is so moderate and pleasant weather now; I was getting real exhausted with the heat. I thought of you too, how it must have exhausted you those hot days. I still occupy the same 3rd story room, 394 L st., and get my breakfast in my room in the morning myself, and dinner at a restaurant about 3 o'clock — I get along very well and very economical (which is a forced put, but just as well). But I must get another room or a boarding-house soon, as the folks are all going to move this month. My good and real friends the O'Connors live in the same block; I am in there every day. Dear mother, tell Mat and Miss Mannahatta I send them my love — I want to see them both. O how I want to see Jeff and you, mother; I sometimes feel as if I should just get in the cars and come home — and the baby too, you must always write about her. Dear mother, good-bye for present. WALT.

XXII

Washington, Sept. 8, 1863, Tuesday morning.
DEAREST MOTHER — I wrote to Jeff Sunday last that his letter sent Sept. 3rd, containing your letter and $5 from Mr. Lane, had miscarried — this morning when I came down to Major Hapgood's office I found it on my table, so it is all right — singular where it has been all this while, as I see the postmark on it is Brooklyn, Sept. 3, as Jeff said. Mother, what to do about Andrew

Letters of 1862-3

I hardly know — as it is I feel about as much pity for you as I do for my poor brother Andrew, for I know you will worry yourself about him all the time. I was in hopes it was only the trouble about the voice, etc., but I see I was mistaken, and it is probably worse. I know you and Jeff and Mat will do all you can — and will have patience with all (it is not only the sick who are poorly off, but their friends; but it is best to have the greatest forbearance, and do and give, etc., whatever one can — but you know that, and practice it too, dear mother). Mother, if I had the means, O how cheerfully I would give them, whether they availed anything for Andrew or not — yet I have long made up my mind that money does not amount to so much, at least not so very much, in serious cases of sickness; it is judgment both in the person himself, and in those he has to do with — and good heart in everything. (Mother, you remember Theodore Gould, how he stuck it out, though sickness and death has had hold of him, as you may say, for fifteen years.) But anyhow, I hope we will all do what we can for Andrew. Mother, I think I must try to come home for a month — I have not given up my project of lecturing I spoke about before, but shall put it in practice yet; I feel clear it will succeed enough. (I wish I had some of the money already; it would be satisfaction to me to contribute something to Andrew's necessities, for he must have bread.) I will write to you, of course, before I come. Mother, I hope you will

The Wound Dresser

live better — Jeff tells me you and Jess and Ed live on poor stuff, you are so economical. Mother, you must n't do so as long as you have a cent — I hope you will, at least four or five times a week, have a steak of beef or mutton, or something substantial for dinner. I have one good meal of that kind every day, or at least five or six days out of the seven — but for breakfast I have nothing but a cup of tea and some bread or crackers (first-rate tea though, with milk and good white sugar). Well, I find it is hearty enough — more than half the time I never eat anything after dinner, and when I do it is only a cracker and cup of tea. Mother, I hope you will not stint yourselves — as to using George's money for your and Jess's and Ed's needful living expenses, I know George would be mad and hurt in his feelings if he thought you was afraid to. Mother, you have a comfortable time as much as you can, and get a steak occasionally, won't you? I suppose Mat got her letter last Saturday; I sent it Friday. O I was so pleased that Jeff was not drawn, and I know how Mat must have felt too; I have no idea the Government will try to draft again, whatever happens — they have carried their point, but have not made much out of it. O how the conscripts and substitutes are deserting down in front and on their way there — you don't hear anything about it, but it is incredible — they don't allow it to get in the papers. Mother, I was so glad to get your letter; you must write again — can't you write to-morrow, so

Letters of 1862-3

I can get it Friday or Saturday? — you know though you wrote more than a week ago I did not get it till this morning. I wish Jeff to write too, as often as he can. Mother, I was gratified to hear you went up among the soldiers — they are rude in appearance, but they know what is decent, and it pleases them much to have folks, even old women, take an interest and come among them. Mother, you must go again, and take Mat. Well, dear mother, I must close. I am first rate in health, so much better than a month and two months ago — my hand has entirely healed. I go to hospital every day or night — I believe no men ever loved each other as I and some of these poor wounded sick and dying men love each other. Good-bye, dearest mother, for present. WALT.

Tuesday afternoon. Mother, it seems to be certain that Meade has gained the day, and that the battles there in Pennsylvania have been about as terrible as any in the war — I think the killed and wounded there on both sides were as many as eighteen or twenty thousand — in one place, four or five acres, there were a thousand dead at daybreak on Saturday morning. Mother, one's heart grows sick of war, after all, when you see what it really is; every once in a while I feel so horrified and disgusted — it seems to me like a great slaughter-house and the men mutually butchering each other — then I feel how impossible it appears, again, to retire from this contest, until we have carried our points (it is cruel to

The Wound Dresser

be so tossed from pillar to post in one's judgment). Washington is a pleasant place in some respects — it has the finest trees, and plenty of them everywhere, on the streets and grounds. The Capitol grounds, though small, have the finest cultivated trees I ever see — there is a great variety, and not one but is in perfect condition. After I finish this letter I am going out there for an hour's recreation. The great sights of Washington are the public buildings, the wide streets, the public grounds, the trees, the Smithsonian institute and grounds. I go to the latter occasionally — the institute is an old fogy concern, but the grounds are fine. Sometimes I go up to Georgetown, about two and a half miles up the Potomac, an old town — just opposite it in the river is an island, where the niggers have their first Washington reg't encamped. They make a good show, are often seen in the streets of Washington in squads. Since they have begun to carry arms, the Secesh here and in Georgetown (about three fifths) are not insulting to them as formerly.

One of the things here always on the go is long trains of army wagons — sometimes they will stream along all day; it almost seems as if there was nothing else but army wagons and ambulances. They have great camps here in every direction, of army wagons, teamsters, ambulance camps, etc.; some of them are permanent, and have small hospitals. I go to them (as no one else goes; ladies would not venture). I sometimes

Letters of 1862-3

have the luck to give some of the drivers a great deal of comfort and help. Indeed, mother, there are camps here of everything—I went once or twice to the contraband camp, to the hospital, etc., but I could not bring myself to go again — when I meet black men or boys among my own hospitals, I use them kindly, give them something, etc. — I believe I told you that I do the same to the wounded Rebels, too — but as there is a limit to one's sinews and endurance and sympathies, etc., I have got in the way, after going lightly, as it were, all through the wards of a hospital, and trying to give a word of cheer, if nothing else, to every one, then confining my special attentions to the few where the investment seems to tell best, and who want it most. Mother, I have real pride in telling you that I have the consciousness of saving quite a number of lives by saving them from giving up — and being a good deal with them; the men say it is so, and the doctors say it is so — and I will candidly confess I can see it is true, though I say it of myself. I know you will like to hear it, mother, so I tell you. I am finishing this in Major Hapgood's office, about 1 o'clock — it is pretty warm, but has not cleared off yet. The trees look so well from where I am, and the Potomac — it is a noble river; I see it several miles, and the Arlington heights. Mother, I see some of the 47th Brooklyn every day or two; the reg't is on the heights back of Arlington house, a fine camp ground. O Matty, I have just thought of you — dear sister, how are you

The Wound Dresser

getting along? Jeff, I will write you truly. Good-bye for the present, dearest mother, and all. WALT.

XXIII

Washington, Sept. 15, 1863. DEAR MOTHER — Your letters were very acceptable — one came just as I was putting my last in the post office — I guess they all come right. I have written to Han and George and sent George papers. Mother, have you heard anything whether the 51st went on with Burnside, or did they remain as a reserve in Kentucky? Burnside has managed splendidly so far, his taking Knoxville and all together — it is a first-class success. I have known Tennessee Union men here in hospital, and I understand it, therefore — the region where Knoxville is is mainly Union, but the Southerners could not exist without it, as it is in their midst, so they determined to pound and kill and crush out the Unionists — all the savage and monstrous things printed in the papers about their treatment are true, at least that kind of thing is, as bad as the Irish in the mob treated the poor niggers in New York. We North don't understand some things about Southerners; it is very strange, the contrast — if I should pick out the most genuine Union men and real patriots I have ever met in all my experience, I should pick out two or three Tennessee and Virginia Unionists I have met in the hospitals, wounded or sick. One

Letters of 1862-3

young man I guess I have mentioned to you in my letters, John Barker, 2nd Tennessee Vol. (Union), was a long while a prisoner in Secesh prisons in Georgia, and in Richmond — three times the devils hung him up by the heels to make him promise to give up his Unionism; once he was cut down for dead. He is a young married man with one child. His little property destroyed, his wife and child turned out — he hunted and tormented — and any moment he could have had anything if he would join the Confederacy — but he was firm as a rock; he would not even take an oath to not fight for either side. They held him about eight months — then he was very sick, scurvy, and they exchanged him and he came up from Richmond here to hospital; here I got acquainted with him. He is a large, slow, good-natured man, somehow made me often think of father; shrewd, very little to say — wouldn't talk to anybody but me. His whole thought was to get back and fight; he was not fit to go, but he has gone back to Tennessee. He spent two days with his wife and young one there, and then to his regiment — he writes to me frequently and I to him; he is not fit to soldier, for the Rebels have destroyed his health and strength (though he is only 23 or 4), but nothing will keep him from his regiment, and fighting — he is uneducated, but as sensible a young man as I ever met, and understands the whole question. Well, mother, Jack Barker is the most genuine Union man I have ever yet met. I asked him once very

The Wound Dresser

gravely why he didn't take the Southern oath and get his liberty — if he didn't think he was foolish to be so stiff, etc. I never saw such a look as he gave me, he thought I was in earnest — the old devil himself couldn't have had put a worse look in his eyes. Mother, I have no doubt there are quite a good many just such men. He is down there with his regiment (one of his brothers was killed) — when he fails in strength he gets the colonel to detach him to do teamster's duty for a few days, on a march till he recruits his strength — but he always carries his gun with him — in a battle he is always in the ranks — then he is so sensible, such decent manly ways, nothing shallow or mean (he must have been a giant in health, but now he is weaker, has a cough too. Mother, can you wonder at my getting so attached to such men, with such love, especially when they show it to me — some of them on their dying beds, and in the very hour of death, or just the same when they recover, or partially recover? I never knew what American young men were till I have been in the hospitals. Well, mother, I have got writing on — there is nothing new with me, just the same old thing, as I suppose it is with you there. Mother, how is Andrew? I wish to hear all about him — I do hope he is better, and that it will not prove anything so bad. I will write to him soon myself, but in the meantime you must tell him to not put so much faith in medicine — drugs, I mean — as in the true curative things ; namely, diet and careful habits, breathing

Letters of 1862-3

good air, etc. You know I wrote in a former letter what is the cause and foundation of the diseases of the throat and what must be the remedy that goes to the bottom of the thing — sudden attacks are to be treated with applications and medicines, but diseases of a seated character are not to be cured by them, only perhaps a little relieved (and often aggravated, made firmer).

Dearest mother, I hope you yourself are well, and getting along good. About the letter in the *Times*, I see ever since I sent they have been very crowded with news that must be printed — I think they will give it yet. I hear there is a new paper in Brooklyn, or to be one — I wish Jeff would send me some of the first numbers without fail, and a stray *Eagle* in same parcel to make up the 4 ounces. I am glad to hear Mat was going to write me a good long letter — every letter from home is so good, when one is away (I often see the men crying in the hospital when they get a letter). Jeff too, I want him to write whenever he can, and not forget the new paper. We are having pleasant weather here; it is such a relief from that awful heat (I can't think of another such siege without feeling sick at the thought).

Mother, I believe I told you I had written to Mrs. Price — do you see Emma? Are the soldiers still on Fort Greene? Well, mother, I have writ quite a letter — it is between 2 and 3 o'clock — I am in Major Hapgood's all alone —

The Wound Dresser

from my window I see all the Potomac, and all around Washington — Major and all gone down to the army to pay troops, and I keep house. I am invited to dinner to-day at 4 o'clock at a Mr. Boyle's — I am going (hope we shall have something good). Dear mother, I send you my love, and some to Jeff and Mat and all, not forgetting Mannahatta (who I hope is a help and comfort to her grandmother). Well, I must scratch off in a hurry, for it is nearly an hour [later] than I thought. Good-bye for the present, dear mother.

WALT.

XXIV

Washington, Sept. 29, 1863. DEAR MOTHER — Well, here I sit this forenoon in a corner by the window in Major Hapgood's office, all the Potomac, and Maryland, and Virginia hills in sight, writing my Tuesday letter to you, dearest mother. Major has gone home to Boston on sick leave, and only the clerk and me occupy the office, and he not much of the time. At the present moment there are two wounded officers come in to get their pay — one has crutches; the other is drest in the light-blue uniform of the invalid corps. Way up here on the 5th floor it is pretty hard scratching for cripples and very weak men to journey up here — often they come up here very weary and faint, and then find out they can't get their money, some red-tape hitch, and the poor soldiers look so disappointed — it always makes me feel bad.

Mother, we are having perfect weather here nowadays, both night and day. The nights are wonderful; for the last three nights as I have walked home from the hospital pretty late, it has seemed to me like a dream, the moon and sky ahead of anything I ever see before. Mother, do you hear anything from George? I wrote to him yesterday and sent him your last letter, and Jeff's enclosed — I shall send him some papers to-day — I send him papers quite often. (Why has n't Jeff sent me the *Union* with my letter in? I want much to see it, and whether they have misprinted it.)

Mother, I don't think the 51st has been in any of the fighting we know of down there yet — what is to come of course nobody can tell. As to Burnside, I suppose you know he is among his *friends*, and I think this quite important, for such the main body of East Tennesseans are, and are far truer Americans anyhow than the Copperheads of the North. The Tennesseans will fight for us too. Mother, you have no idea how the soldiers, sick, etc. (I mean the American ones, to a man) all feel about the Copperheads; they never speak of them without a curse, and I hear them say, with an air that shows they mean it, they would shoot them sooner than they would a Rebel. Mother, the troops from Meade's army are passing through here night and day, going West and so down to reinforce Rosecrans I sup-

The Wound Dresser

pose — the papers are not permitted to mention it, but it is so. Two Army Corps, I should think, have mostly passed — they go through night and day — I hear the whistle of the locomotive screaming away any time at night when I wake up, and the rumbling of the trains.

Mother dear, you must write to me soon, and so must Jeff. I thought Mat was going to send me a great long letter — I am always looking for it; I hope it will be full of everything about family matters and doings, and how everybody really is. I go to Major's box three or four times a day. I want to hear also about Andrew, and indeed about every one of you and everything — nothing is too trifling, nothing uninteresting.

O mother, who do you think I got a letter from, two or three days ago? Aunt Fanny, Ansel's mother — she sent it by a young man, a wounded soldier who has been home to Farmingdale on furlough, and lately returned. She writes a first-rate letter, Quaker all over — I shall answer it. She says Mary and Ansel and all are well. I have received another letter from Mrs. Price — she has not good health. I am sorry for her from my heart; she is a good, noble woman, no better kind. Mother, I am in the hospitals as usual — I stand it better the last three weeks than ever before — I go among the worst fevers and wounds with impunity. I go among the smallpox, etc., just the same — I feel to go without apprehension, and so I go. Nobody else goes; and as the darkey said there at Charleston

Letters of 1862-3

when the boat run on a flat and the Reb sharpshooters were peppering them, "somebody must jump in de water and shove de boat off."

WALT.

XXV

Washington, Oct. 6, 1863. DEAREST MOTHER — Your letter and George's came safe — dear brother George, one don't more than get a letter from him before you want to hear again, especially as things are looking pretty stormy that way — but mother, I rather lean to the opinion that the 51st is still in Kentucky, at or near where George last wrote; but of course that is only my guess. I send George papers and occasionally letters. Mother, I sent him enclosed your letter before the last, though you said in it not to tell him how much money he had home, as you wanted to surprise him; but I sent it. Mother, I think Rosecrans and Burnside will be too much for the Rebels down there yet. I myself make a great acc't of Burnside being in the midst of *friends*, and such friends too — they will fight and fight up to the handle, and kill somebody (it seems as if it was coming to that pass where we will either have to destroy or be destroyed). Mother, I wish you would write soon after you get this, or Jeff or Mat must, and tell me about Andrew, if there is anything different with him — I think about him every day and night. I believe I must come

The Wound Dresser

home, even if it is only for a week — I want to see you all very much. Mother, I know you must have a great deal to harass and trouble you; I don't mean about Andrew personally, for I know you would feel to give your life to save his, and do anything to nourish him, but about the children and Nancy — but, mother, you must not let anything chafe you, and you must not be squeamish about saying firmly at times not to have little Georgy too much to trouble you (poor little fellow, I have no doubt he will be a pleasanter child when he grows older); and while you are pleasant with Nancy you must be sufficiently plain with her — only, mother, I know you will, and Jeff and Mat will too, be invariably good to Andrew, and not mind his being irritable at times; it is his disease, and then his temper is naturally fretful, but it is such a misfortune to have such sickness — and always do anything for him that you can in reason. Mat, my dear sister, I know you will, for I know your nature is to come out a first-class girl in times of trouble and sickness, and do anything. Mother, you don't know how pleased I was to read what you wrote about little Sis. I want to see her so bad I don't know what to do; I know she must be just the best young one on Long Island — but I hope it will not be understood as meaning any slight or disrespect to Miss Hat, nor to put her nose out of joint, because Uncle Walt, I hope, has heart and gizzard big enough for both his little nieces and as many more as the Lord may send.

Letters of 1862-3

Mother, I am writing this in Major Hapgood's office, as usual. I am all alone to-day — Major is still absent, unwell, and the clerk is away somewhere. O how pleasant it is here — the weather I mean — and other things too, for that matter. I still occupy my little room, 394 L st.; get my own breakfast there; had good tea this morning, and some nice biscuit (yesterday morning and day before had peaches cut up). My friends the O'Connors that I wrote about recommenced cooking the 1st of this month (they have been, as usual in summer, taking their meals at a family hotel near by). Saturday they sent for me to breakfast, and Sunday I eat dinner with them — very good dinner, roast beef, lima beans, good potatoes, etc. They are truly friends to me. I still get my dinner at a restaurant usually. I have a very good plain dinner, which is the only meal of any account I make during the day; but it is just as well, for I would be in danger of getting fat on the least encouragement, and I have no ambition that way. Mother, it is lucky I like Washington in many respects, and that things are upon the whole pleasant personally, for every day of my life I see enough to make one's heart ache with sympathy and anguish here in the hospitals, and I do not know as I could stand it if it was not counterbalanced outside. It is curious, when I am present at the most appalling things — deaths, operations, sickening wounds (perhaps full of maggots) — I do not fail, although my sympathies are very much excited, but keep singularly

The Wound Dresser

cool; but often hours afterward, perhaps when I am home or out walking alone, I feel sick and actually tremble when I recall the thing and have it in my mind again before me. Mother, did you see my letter in the N. Y. *Times* of Sunday, Oct. 4? That was the long-delayed letter. Mother, I am very sorry Jeff did not send me the *Union* with my letter in — I wish very much he could do so yet; and always when I have a letter in a paper I would like to have one sent. If you take the *Union*, send me some once in a while. Mother, was it Will Brown sent me those? Tell him if so I was much obliged; and if he or Mr. and Mrs. Brown take any interest in hearing my scribblings, mother, you let them read the letters, of course. O, I must not close without telling you the highly important intelligence that I have cut my hair and beard — since the event Rosecrans, Charleston, etc., etc., have among my acquaintances been hardly mentioned, being insignificant themes in comparison. Jeff, my dearest brother, I have been going to write you a good gossipy letter for two or three weeks past; will try to yet, so it will reach you for Sunday reading — so good-bye, Jeff, and good-bye for present, mother dear, and all, and tell Andrew he must not be discouraged yet. WALT.

Letters of 1862–3

XXVI

Washington, Oct. 11, 1863. DEAR FRIEND[1]— Your letters were both received, and were indeed welcome. Don't mind my not answering them promptly, for you know what a wretch I am about such things. But you must write just as often as you conveniently can. Tell me all about your folks, especially the girls, and about Mr. A. Of course you won't forget Arthur,[2] and always when you write to him send my love. Tell me about Mrs. U. and the dear little rogues. Tell Mrs. B. she ought to be here, hospital matron, only it is a harder pull than folks anticipate. You wrote about Emma;[3] she thinks she might and ought to come as nurse for the soldiers. Dear girl, I know it would be a blessed thing for the men to have her loving spirit and hand, and whoever of the poor fellows had them would indeed think it so. But, my darling, it is a dreadful thing — you don't know these wounds, sickness, etc., the sad condition in which many of the men are brought here, and remain for days; sometimes the wounds full of crawling corruption, etc. Down in the field-hospitals in front they have no proper care (can't have), and after a battle go for many days unattended to.

[1] Mrs. Abby Price, an intimate friend of Whitman, and a friend and neighbor of his mother.
[2] Mrs. Price's son, a naval officer.
[3] Mrs. Price's daughter, and sister of the Helen mentioned later.

The Wound Dresser

Abby, I think often about you and the pleasant days, the visits I used to pay you, and how good it was always to be made so welcome. O, I wish I could come in this afternoon and have a good tea with you, and have three or four hours of mutual comfort, and rest and talk, and be all of us together again. Is Helen home and well? and what is she doing now? And you, my dear friend, how sorry I am to hear that your health is not rugged — but, dear Abby, you must not dwell on anticipations of the worst (but I know that is not your nature, or did not use to be). I hope this will find you quite well and in good spirits. I feel so well myself — I will have to come and see you, I think — I am so fat, out considerable in the open air, and all red and tanned worse than ever. You see, therefore, that my life amid these sad and death-stricken hospitals has not told upon me, for I am this fall so running over with health, and I feel as if I ought to go on, on that account, working among all the sick and deficient; and O how gladly I would bestow upon you a liberal share of my health, dear Abby, if such a thing were possible.

I am continually moving around among the hospitals. One I go to oftenest the last three months is "Armory-square," as it is large, generally full of the worst wounds and sickness, and is among the least visited. To this or some other I never miss a day or evening. I am enabled to give the men something, and perhaps

Letters of 1862–3

some trifle to their supper all around. Then there are always special cases calling for something special. Above all the poor boys welcome magnetic friendship, personality (some are so fervent, so hungering for this) — poor fellows, how young they are, lying there with their pale faces, and that mute look in their eyes. O, how one gets to love them — often, particular cases, so suffering, so good, so manly and affectionate! Abby, you would all smile to see me among them — many of them like children. Ceremony is mostly discarded — they suffer and get exhausted and so weary — not a few are on their dying beds — lots of them have grown to expect, as I leave at night, that we should kiss each other, sometimes quite a number; I have to go round, poor boys. There is little petting in a soldier's life in the field, but, Abby, I know what is in their hearts, always waiting, though they may be unconscious of it themselves.

I have a place where I buy very nice homemade biscuits, sweet crackers, etc. Among others, one of my ways is to get a good lot of these, and, for supper, go through a couple of wards and give a portion to each man — next day two wards more, and so on. Then each marked case needs something to itself. I spend my evenings altogether at the hospitals — my days often. I give little gifts of money in small sums, which I am enabled to do — all sorts of things indeed, food, clothing, letter-stamps (I write lots of letters), now and then a good pair of crutches, etc., etc.

The Wound Dresser

Then I read to the boys. The whole ward that can walk gathers around me and listens.

All this I tell you, my dear, because I know it will interest you. I like Washington very well. (Did you see my last letter in the New York *Times* of October 4th, Sunday?) I have three or four hours' work every day copying, and in writing letters for the press, etc.; make enough to pay my way — live in an inexpensive manner anyhow. I like the mission I am on here, and as it deeply holds me I shall continue.

October 15. Well, Abby, I guess I send you letter enough. I ought to have finished and sent off the letter last Sunday, when it was written. I have been pretty busy. We are having new arrivals of wounded and sick now all the time — some very bad cases. Abby, should you come across any one who feels to help contribute to the men through me, write me. (I may then send word some purchases I should find acceptable for the men). But this only if it happens to come in that you know or meet any one, perfectly convenient. Abby, I have found some good friends here, a few, but true as steel — W. D. O'Connor and wife above all. He is a clerk in the Treasury — she is a Yankee girl. Then C. W. Eldridge[1] in Paymaster's Department. He is a Boston boy, too — their friendship has been unswerving.

In the hospitals, among these American young men, I could not describe to you what mutual

---

[1] Formerly of Thayer & Eldridge, the first Boston publishers of "Leaves of Grass" (1860 Edition).

Letters of 1862-3

attachments, and how passing deep and tender these boys. Some have died, but the love for them lives as long as I draw breath. These soldiers know how to love too, when once they have the right person and the right love offered them. It is wonderful. You see I am running off into the clouds, but this is my element. Abby, I am writing this note this afternoon in Major H's office — he is away sick — I am here a good deal of the time alone. It is a dark rainy afternoon — we don't know what is going on down in front, whether Meade is getting the worst of it or not — (but the result of the big elections cheers us). I believe fully in Lincoln — few know the rocks and quicksands he has to steer through. I enclose you a note Mrs. O'C. handed me to send you — written, I suppose, upon impulse. She is a noble Massachusetts woman, is not very rugged in health — I am there very much — her husband and I are great friends too. Well, I will close — the rain is pouring, the sky leaden, it is between 2 and 3. I am going to get some dinner, and then to the hospital. Good-bye, dear friends, and I send my love to all.

WALT WHITMAN.

XXVII

Washington, Oct. 13, 1863. DEAREST MOTHER — Nothing particular new with me. I am well and hearty — think a good deal about home. Mother,

The Wound Dresser

I so much want to see you, even if only for a couple of weeks, for I feel I must return here and continue my hospital operations. They are so much needed, although one can do only such a little in comparison, amid these thousands. Then I desire much to see Andrew. I wonder if I could cheer him up any. Does he get any good from that treatment with the baths, etc.? Mother, I suppose you have your hands full with Nancy's poor little children, and one worry and another (when one gets old little things bother a great deal). Mother, I go down every day looking for a letter from you or Jeff — I had two from Jeff latter part of the week. I want to see Jeff much. I wonder why he did n't send me the *Union* with my letter in; I am disappointed at not getting it. I sent Han a N. Y. *Times* with my last letter, and one to George too. Have you heard anything from George or Han? There is a new lot of wounded now again. They have been arriving sick and wounded for three days — first long strings of ambulances with the sick, but yesterday many with bad and bloody wounds, poor fellows. I thought I was cooler and more used to it, but the sight of some of them brought tears into my eyes. Mother, I had the good luck yesterday to do quite a great deal of good. I had provided a lot of nourishing things for the men, but for another quarter — but I had them where I could use them immediately for these new wounded as they came in faint and hungry, and fagged out with a long rough journey, all

Letters of 1862-3

dirty and torn, and many pale as ashes and all bloody. I distributed all my stores, gave partly to the nurses I knew that were just taking charge of them — and as many as I could I fed myself. Then besides I found a lot of oyster soup handy, and I procured it all at once. Mother, it is the most pitiful sight, I think, when first the men are brought in. I have to bustle round, to keep from crying — they are such rugged young men — all these just arrived are cavalry men. Our troops got the worst of it, but fought like devils. Our men engaged were Kilpatrick's Cavalry. They were in the rear as part of Meade's retreat, and the Reb cavalry cut in between and cut them off and attacked them and shelled them terribly. But Kilpatrick brought them out mostly — this was last Sunday.

Mother, I will try to come home before long, if only for six or eight days. I wish to see you, and Andrew — I wish to see the young ones; and Mat, you must write. I am about moving. I have been hunting for a room to-day — I shall [write] next [time] how I succeed. Good-bye for present, dear mother. WALT.

XXVIII

Washington, Oct. 20, 1863. DEAREST MOTHER — I got your last letter Sunday morning, though it was dated Thursday night. Mother, I suppose you got a letter from me Saturday last, as

The Wound Dresser

I sent one the day before, as I was concerned about Andrew. If I thought it would be any benefit to Andrew I should certainly leave everything else and come back to Brooklyn. Mother, do you recollect what I wrote last summer about throat diseases, when Andrew was first pretty bad? Well, that's the whole groundwork of the business; any true physician would confirm it. There is no great charm about such things; as to any costly and mysterious baths, there are no better baths than warm water, or vapor (and perhaps sulphur vapor). There is nothing costly or difficult about them; one can have a very good sweating bath, at a pinch, by having a pan of warm water under a chair with a couple of blankets around him to enclose the vapor, and heating a couple of bricks or stones or anything to put in one after another, and sitting on the chair — it is a very wholesome sweat, too, and not to be sneezed at if one wishes to do what is salutary, and thinks of the sense of a thing, and not what others do. Andrew mustn't be discouraged; those diseases are painful and tedious, but he can recover, and will yet. Dear mother, I sent your last letter to George, with a short one I wrote myself. I sent it yesterday. I sent a letter last Wednesday (14th) to him also, hoping that if one don't reach him another will. Hasn't Jeff seen Capt. Sims or Lieut. McReady yet, and don't they hear whether the 51st is near Nicholasville, Kentucky, yet? I send George papers now and then. Mother, one of your letters contains

Letters of 1862-3

part of my letter to the *Union* (I wish I could have got the whole of it). It seems to me mostly as I intended it, barring a few slight misprints. Was my last name signed at the bottom of it? Tell me when you write next. Dear mother, I am real sorry, and mad too, that the water works people have cut Jeff's wages down to $50; this is a pretty time to cut a man's wages down, the mean old punkin heads. Mother, I can't understand it at all; tell me more of the particulars. Jeff, I often wish you was on here; you would be better appreciated — there are big salaries paid here sometimes to civil engineers. Jeff, I know a fellow, E. C. Stedman; has been here till lately; is now in Wall street. He is poor, but he is in with the big bankers, Hallett & Co., who are in with Fremont in his line of Pacific railroad. I can get his (Stedman's) address, and should you wish it any time I will give you a letter to him. I should n't wonder if the big men, with Fremont at head, were going to push their route works, road, etc., etc., in earnest, and if a fellow could get a good managing place in it, why it might be worth while. I think after Jeff has been with the Brooklyn w[ater] w[orks] from the beginning, and so faithful and so really valuable, to put down to $50 — the mean, low-lived old shoats! I have felt as indignant about it, the meanness of the thing, and mighty inconvenient, too — $40 a month makes a big difference. Mother, I hope Jeff won't get and keep himself in a perpetual fever, with all these things and others and

The Wound Dresser

botherations, both family and business ones. If he does, he will just wear himself down before his time comes. I do hope, Jeff, you will take things equally all round, and not brood or think too deeply. So I go on giving you all good advice. O mother, I must tell you how I get along in my new quarters. I have moved to a new room, 456 Sixth street, not far from Pennsylvania avenue (the big street here), and not far from the Capitol. It is in the 3d story, an addition back; seems to be going to prove a very good winter room, as it is right under the roof and looks south; has low windows, is plenty big enough; I have gas. I think the lady will prove a good woman. She is old and feeble. (There is a little girl of 4 or 5; I hear her sometimes calling *Grandma, Grandma,* just exactly like Hat; it made me think of you and Hat right away.) One thing is I am quite by myself; there is no passage up there except to my room, and right off against my side of the house is a great old yard with grass and some trees back, and the sun shines in all day, etc., and it smells sweet, and good air — good big bed; I sleep first rate. There is a young wench of 12 or 13, Lucy (the niggers here are the best and most amusing creatures you ever see) — she comes and goes, gets water, etc. She is pretty much the only one I see. Then I believe the front door is not locked at all at night. (In the other place the old thief, the landlord, had two front doors, with four locks and bolts on one and three on the other — and a

Letters of 1862-3

big bulldog in the back yard. We were well fortified, I tell you. Sometimes I had an awful time at night getting in.) I pay $10 a month; this includes gas, but not fuel. Jeff, you can come on and see me easy now. Mother, to give you an idea of prices here, while I was looking for rooms, about like our two in Wheeler's houses (2nd story), nothing extra about them, either in location or anything, and the rent was $60 a month. Yet, quite curious, vacant houses here are not so very dear; very much the same as in Brooklyn. Dear mother, Jeff wrote in his letter latter part of last week, you was real unwell with a very bad cold (and that you did n't have enough good meals). Mother, I hope this will find you well and in good spirits. I think about you every day and night. Jeff thinks you show your age more, and failing like. O my dear mother, you must not think of failing yet. I hope we shall have some comfortable years yet. Mother, don't allow things, troubles, to take hold of you; write a few lines whenever you can; tell me exactly how things are. Mother, I am first rate and well — only a little of that deafness again. Good-bye for present. WALT.

XXIX

Washington, Oct. 27, 1863. DEAREST MOTHER, — Yours and George's letter came, and a letter from Jeff too — all good. I had received a letter a day

The Wound Dresser

or so before from George too. I am very glad he is at Camp Nelson, Kentucky, and I hope and pray the reg't will be kept there — for God knows they have tramped enough for the last two years, and fought battles and been through enough. I have sent George papers to Camp Nelson, and will write to-morrow. I send him the *Unions* and the late New York papers. Mother, you or Jeff write and tell me how Andrew is; I hope he will prove to be better. Such complaints are sometimes very alarming for awhile, and then take such a turn for the better. Common means and steadily pursuing them, about diet especially, are so much more reliable than any course of medicine whatever. Mother, I have written to Han; I sent her George's letter to me, and wrote her a short letter myself. I sent it four or five days ago. Mother, I am real pleased to hear Jeff's explanation how it is that his wages is cut down, and that it was not as I fancied from the meanness of the old coons in the board. I felt so indignant about it, as I took it into my head, (though I don't know why) that it was done out of meanness, and was a sort of insult. I was quite glad Jeff wrote a few lines about it — and glad they appreciate Jeff, too. Mother, if any of my soldier boys should ever call upon you (as they are often anxious to have my address in Brooklyn) you just use them as you know how to without ceremony, and if you happen to have pot luck and feel to ask them to take a bite, don't be afraid to do so. There is

Letters of 1862–3

one very good boy, Thos. Neat, 2nd N. Y. Cavalry, wounded in leg. He is now home on furlough — his folks live, I think, in Jamaica. He is a noble boy. He may call upon you. (I gave him here $1 toward buying his crutches, etc.) I like him very much. Then possibly a Mr. Haskell, or some of his folks from Western New York, may call — he had a son died here, a very fine boy. I was with him a good deal, and the old man and his wife have written me, and asked me my address in Brooklyn. He said he had children in N. Y. city and was occasionally down there. Mother, when I come home I will show you some of the letters I get from mothers, sisters, fathers, etc. — they will make you cry. There is nothing new with my hospital doings — I was there yesterday afternoon and evening, and shall be there again to-day. Mother, I should like to hear how you are yourself — has your cold left you, and do you feel better? Do you feel quite well again? I suppose you have your good stove all fired up these days — we have had some real cool weather here. I must rake up a little cheap second-hand stove for my room, for it was in the bargain that I should get that myself. Mother, I like my place quite well, better on nearly every account than my old room, but I see it will only do for a winter room. They keep it clean, and the house smells clean, and the room too. My old room, they just let everything lay where it was, and you can fancy what a litter of dirt there was — still

The Wound Dresser

it was a splendid room for air, for summer, as good as there is in Washington. I got a letter from Mrs. Price this morning — does Emmy ever come to see you?

Matty, my dear sister, and Miss Mannahatta, and the little one (whose name I don't know, and perhaps has n't got any name yet), I hope you are all well and having good times. I often, often think about you all. Mat, do you go any to the Opera now? They say the new singers are so good — when I come home we'll try to go. Mother, I am very well — have some cold in my head and my ears stopt up yet, making me sometimes quite hard of hearing. I am writing this in Major Hapgood's office. Last Sunday I took dinner at my friends the O'Connors — had two roast chickens, stewed tomatoes, potatoes, etc. I took dinner there previous Sunday also.

Well, dear mother, how the time passes away — to think it will soon be a year I have been away! It has passed away very swiftly, somehow, to me. O what things I have witnessed during that time — I shall never forget them. And the war is not settled yet, and one does not see anything at all certain about the settlement yet; but I have finally got for good, I think, into the feeling that our triumph is assured, whether it be sooner or whether it be later, or whatever roundabout way we are led there, and I find I don't change that conviction from any reverses we meet, or any delays or Government blunders. There are

Letters of 1862-3

blunders enough, heaven knows, but I am thankful things have gone on as well for us as they have — thankful the ship rides safe and sound at all. Then I have finally made up my mind that Mr. Lincoln has done as good as a human man could do. I still think him a pretty big President. I realize here in Washington that it has been a big thing to have just kept the United States from being thrown down and having its throat cut; and now I have no doubt it will throw down Secession and cut its throat — and I have not had any doubt since Gettysburg. Well, dear, dear mother, I will draw to a close. Andrew and Jeff and all, I send you my love. Good-bye, dear mother and dear Matty and all hands. WALT.

XXX

Washington, Dec. 15, 1863. DEAREST MOTHER — The last word I got from home was your letter written the night before Andrew was buried — Friday night, nearly a fortnight ago. I have not heard anything since from you or Jeff. Mother, Major Hapgood has moved from his office, cor. 15th street, and I am not with him any more. He has moved his office to his private room. I am writing this in my room, 456 Sixth street, but my letters still come to Major's care; they are to be addrest same as ever, as I can easily go and get them out of his box (only nothing

The Wound Dresser

need be sent me any time to the old office, as I am not there, nor Major either). Anything like a telegraphic dispatch or express box or the like should be addrest 456 Sixth street, 3rd story, back room. Dear mother, I hope you are well and in good spirits. I wish you would try to write to me everything about home and the particulars of Andrew's funeral, and how you all are getting along. I have not received the *Eagle* with the little piece in. I was in hopes Jeff would have sent it. I wish he would yet, or some of you would; I want to see it. I think it must have been put in by a young man named Howard; he is now editor of the *Eagle*, and is very friendly to me.

Mother, I am quite well. I have been out this morning early, went down through the market; it is quite a curiosity — I bought some butter, tea, etc. I have had my breakfast here in my room, good tea, bread and butter, etc.

Mother, I think about you all more than ever — and poor Andrew, I often think about him. Mother, write to me how Nancy and the little boys are getting along. I got thinking last night about little California.[1] O how I wished I had her here for an hour to take care of — dear little girl. I don't think I ever saw a young one I took to so much — but I must n't slight Hattie; I like her too. Mother, I am still going among the hospitals; there is plenty of need, just the same as ever. I go every day or evening. I have not

[1] Jeff's daughter Jessie was originally called California.

Letters of 1862–3

heard from George — I have no doubt the 51st is still at Crab Orchard.

Mother, I hope you will try to write. I send you my love, and to Jeff and Mat and all — so good-bye, dear mother. WALT.

LETTERS OF 1864

I

WASHINGTON, *Friday afternoon, Jan. 29. '64.* DEAR MOTHER — Your letter of Tuesday night came this forenoon — the one of Sunday night I received yesterday. Mother, you don't say in either of them whether George has re-enlisted or not — or is that not yet decided positively one way or the other?

O mother, how I should like to be home (I don't want more than two or three days). I want to see George (I have his photograph on the wall, right over my table all the time), and I want to see California — you must always write in your letters how she is. I shall write to Han this afternoon or to-morrow morning and tell her probably George will come out and see her, and that if he does you will send her word beforehand.

Jeff, my dear brother, if there should be the change made in the works, and things all overturned, you must n't mind — I dare say you will pitch into something better. I believe a real overturn in the dead old beaten track of a man's life, especially a young man's, is always likely to turn out best, though it worries one at first dreadfully. Mat, I want to see you most sincerely — they have n't put in anything in the last two or three letters about you, but I suppose you are well, my dear sister.

The Wound Dresser

Mother, the young man that I took care of, Lewis Brown, is pretty well, but very restless — he is doing well now, but there is a long road before him yet; it is torture for him to be tied so to his cot, this weather; he is a very noble young man and has suffered very much. He is a Maryland boy and (like the Southerners when they *are* Union) I think he is as strong and resolute a Union boy as there is in the United States. He went out in a Maryland reg't, but transferred to a N. Y. battery. But I find so many noble men in the ranks I have ceased to wonder at it. I think the soldiers from the New England States and the Western States are splendid, and the country parts of N. Y. and Pennsylvania too. I think less of the great cities than I used to. I know there are black sheep enough even in the ranks, but the general rule is the soldiers are noble, very.

Mother, I wonder if George thinks as I do about the best way to enjoy a visit home, after all. When I come home again, I shall not go off gallivanting with my companions half as much nor a quarter as much as I used to, but shall spend the time quietly home with you while I do stay; it is a great humbug spreeing around, and a few choice friends for a man, the real right kind in a quiet way, are enough.

Mother, I hope you take things easy, don't you? Mother, you know I was always advising you to let things go and sit down and take what comfort you can while you do live. It is very

Letters of 1864

warm here; this afternoon it is warm enough for July — the sun burns where it shines on your face; it is pretty dusty in the principal streets.

Congress is in session; I see Odell, Kalbfleisch, etc., often. I have got acquainted with Mr. Garfield, an M. C. from Ohio, and like him very much indeed (he has been a soldier West, and I believe a good brave one — was a major general). I don't go much to the debates this session yet. Congress will probably keep in session till well into the summer. As to what course things will take, political or military, there's no telling. I think, though, the Secesh military power is getting more and more shaky. How they can make any headway against our new, large, and fresh armies next season passes my wit to see.

Mother, I was talking with a pretty high officer here, who is behind the scenes — I was mentioning that I had a great desire to be present at a first-class battle; he told me if I would only stay around here three or four weeks longer my wish would probably be gratified. I asked him what he meant, what he alluded to specifically, but he would not say anything further — so I remain as much in the dark as before — only there seemed to be some meaning in his remark, and it was made to me only as there was no one else in hearing at the moment (he is quite an admirer of my poetry).

The re-enlistment of the veterans is the greatest thing yet; it pleases everybody but the Rebels —

The Wound Dresser

and surprises everybody too. Mother, I am well and fat (I must weigh about 206), so Washington must agree with me. I work three or four hours a day copying. Dear mother, I send you and Hattie my love, as you say she is a dear little girl. Mother, try to write every week, even if only a few lines. Love to George and Jeff and Mat. WALT.

II

Washington, Feb. 2, 1864. DEAREST MOTHER — I am writing this by the side of the young man you asked about, Lewis Brown in Armory-square hospital. He is getting along very well indeed — the amputation is healing up good, and he does not suffer anything like as much as he did. I see him every day. We have had real hot weather here, and for the last three days wet and rainy; it is more like June than February. Mother, I wrote to Han last Saturday — she must have got it yesterday. I have not heard anything from home since a week ago (your last letter). I suppose you got a letter from me Saturday last. I am well as usual. There has been several hundred sick soldiers brought in here yesterday. I have been around among them to-day all day — it is enough to make me heart-sick, the old times over again; they are many of them mere wrecks, though young men (sickness is worse in some respects than wounds).

Letters of 1864

One boy about 16, from Portland, Maine, only came from home a month ago, a recruit; he is here now very sick and down-hearted, poor child. He is a real country boy; I think has consumption. He was only a week with his reg't. I sat with him a long time; I saw [it] did him great good. I have been feeding some their dinners. It makes me feel quite proud, I find so frequently I can do with the men what no one else at all can, getting them to eat (some that will not touch their food otherwise, nor for anybody else) — it is sometimes quite affecting, I can tell you. I found such a case to-day, a soldier with throat disease, very bad. I fed him quite a dinner; the men, his comrades around, just stared in wonder, and one of them told me afterwards that he (the sick man) had not eat so much at a meal in three months. Mother, I shall have my hands pretty full now for a while — write all about things home. WALT.

Lewis Brown says I must give you his love — he says he knows he would like you if he should see you.

III

Washington, Friday afternoon, Feb. 5, 1864.
DEAREST MOTHER — I am going down in front, in the midst of the army, to-morrow morning, to be gone for about a week — so I thought I would write you a few lines now, to let you know.

Mother, I suppose you got my letter written

The Wound Dresser

last Tuesday — I have not got any from home now for a number of days. I am well and hearty. The young man Lewis Brown is able to be up a little on crutches. There is quite a number of sick young men I have taken in hand, from the late arrivals, that I am sorry to leave. Sick and down-hearted and lonesome, they think so much of a friend, and I get so attached to them too — but I want to go down in camp once more very much ; and I think I shall be back in a week. I shall spend most of my time among the sick and wounded in the camp hospitals. If I had means I should stop with them, poor boys, or go among them periodically, dispensing what I had, as long as the war lasts, down among the worst of it (although what are collected here in hospital seem to me about as severe and needy cases as any, after all).

Mother, I want to hear about you all, and about George and how he is spending his time home. Mother, I do hope you are well and in good spirits, and Jeff and Mat and all, and dear little California and Hattie — I send them all my love. Mother, I may write to you from down in front — so good-bye, dear mother, for present.   WALT.

I hope I shall find several letters waiting for me when I get back here.

Letters of 1864

IV

Culpepper, Virginia, Friday night, Feb. 12, 1864.
DEAREST MOTHER — I am still stopping down in this region. I am a good deal of the time down within half a mile of our picket lines, so that you see I can indeed call myself in the front. I stopped yesterday with an artillery camp in the 1st Corps at the invitation of Capt. Crawford, who said that he knew me in Brooklyn. It is close to the lines — I asked him if he did not think it dangerous. He said, No, he could have a large force of infantry to help him there, in very short metre, if there was any sudden emergency. The troops here are scattered all around, much more apart than they seemed to me to be opposite Fredericksburg last winter. They mostly have good huts and fireplaces, etc. I have been to a great many of the camps, and I must say I am astonished [how] good the houses are almost everywhere. I have not seen one regiment, nor any part of one, in the poor uncomfortable little shelter tents that I saw so common last winter after Fredericksburg — but all the men have built huts of logs and mud. A good many of them would be comfortable enough to live in under any circumstances. I have been in the division hospitals around here. There are not many men sick here, and no wounded — they now send them on to Washington. I shall return there in a few days, as I am very clear that the real need of one's services is there after all — there the worst cases concentrate, and

The Wound Dresser

probably will, while the war lasts. I suppose you know that what we call hospital here in the field is nothing but a collection of tents on the bare ground for a floor — rather hard accommodation for a sick man. They heat them there by digging a long trough in the ground under them, covering it over with old railroad iron and earth, and then building a fire at one end and letting it draw through and go out at the other, as both ends are open. This heats the ground through the middle of the hospital quite hot. I find some poor creatures crawling about pretty weak with diarrhœa; there is a great deal of that; they keep them until they get very bad indeed, and then send them to Washington. This aggravates the complaint, and they come into Washington in a terrible condition. O mother, how often and how many I have seen come into Washington from this awful complaint after such an experience as I have described — with the look of death on their poor young faces; they keep them so long in the field hospitals with poor accommodations the disease gets too deeply seated.

To-day I have been out among some of the camps of the 2nd division of the 1st Corps. I have been wandering around all day, and have had a very good time, over woods, hills, and gullies — indeed, a real soldier's march. The weather is good and the travelling quite tolerable. I have been in the camps of some Massachusetts, Pennsylvania, and New York regiments. I have friends in them, and went out to see them, and see sol-

Letters of 1864

diering generally, as I can never cease to crave more and more knowledge of actual soldiers' life, and to be among them as much as possible. This evening I have also been in a large wagoners' camp. They had good fires and were very cheerful. I went to see a friend there, too, but did not find him in. It is curious how many I find that I know and that know me. Mother, I have no difficulty at all in making myself at home among the soldiers, teamsters, or any — I most always find they like to have me very much; it seems to do them good. No doubt they soon feel that my heart and sympathies are truly with them, and it is both a novelty and pleases them and touches their feelings, and so doubtless does them good — and I am sure it does that to me. There is more fun around here than you would think for. I told you about the theatre the 14th Brooklyn has got up — they have songs and burlesques, etc.; some of the performers real good. As I write this I have heard in one direction or another two or three good bands playing — and hear one tooting away some gay tunes now, though it is quite late at night. Mother, I don't know whether I mentioned in my last letter that I took dinner with Col. Fowler one day early part of the week. His wife is stopping here. I was down at the 14th as I came along this evening, too — one of the officers told me about a presentation to George of a sword, etc. — he said he see it in the papers. The 14th invited me to come and be their guest while I staid here, but I have not been able to accept.

The Wound Dresser

Col. Fowler uses me tip-top — he is provost marshal of this region; makes a good officer. Mother, I could get no pen and ink to-night. Well, dear mother, I send you my love, and to George and Jeff and Mat and little girls and all. WALT.

Direct to care of Major Hapgood as before, and write soon. Mother, I suppose you got a letter I wrote from down here last Monday.

V

Washington, March 2, 1864. DEAR MOTHER — You or Jeff must try to write as soon as you receive this and let me know how little Sis is. Tell me if she got entirely over the croup and how she is — also about George's trunks. I do hope he received them; it was such a misfortune; I want to hear the end of it; I am in hopes I shall hear that he has got them. I have not seen in the papers whether the 51st has left New York yet. Mother, I want to hear all about home and all the occurrences, especially the two things I have just mentioned, and how you are, for somehow I was thinking from your letters lately whether you was as well as usual or not. Write how my dear sister Mat is too, and whether you are still going to stay there in Portland avenue the coming year. Well, dear mother, I am just the same here — nothing new. I am well and hearty, and constantly moving around among the wounded and sick. There are a great many of the latter com-

Letters of 1864

ing up — the hospitals here are quite full — lately they have [been] picking out in the hospitals all that had pretty well recovered, and sending them back to their regiments. They seem to be determined to strengthen the army this spring to the utmost. They are sending down many to their reg'ts that are not fit to go in my opinion — then there are squads and companies, and reg'ts, too, passing through here in one steady stream, going down to the front, returning from furlough home; but then there are quite a number leaving the army on furlough, re-enlisting, and going North for a while. They pass through here quite largely. Mother, Lewis Brown is getting quite well; he will soon be able to have a wooden leg put on. He is very restless and active, and wants to go round all the time. Sam Beatty is here in Washington. We have had quite a snow storm, but [it] is clear and sunny to-day here, but sloshy. I am wearing my army boots — anything but the dust. Dear mother, I want to see you and Sis and Mat and all very much. If I can get a chance I think I shall come home for a while. I want to try to bring out a book of poems, a new one, to be called "Drum-Taps," and I want to come to New York for that purpose, too.

Mother, I have n't given up the project of lecturing, either, but whatever I do, I shall for the main thing devote myself for years to come to these wounded and sick, what little I can. Well, good-bye, dear mother, for present — write soon. W<small>ALT</small>.

The Wound Dresser

VI

Washington, March 15, 1864. DEAREST MOTHER — I got a letter from Jeff last Sunday — he says you have a very bad cold indeed. Dear mother, I feel very much concerned about it; I do hope it has passed over before this. Jeff wrote me about the house. I hope it will be so you can both remain in the same house; it would be much more satisfaction. . . . The poor boy very sick of brain fever I was with, is dead; he was only 19 and a noble boy, so good though out of his senses some eight days, though still having a kind of idea of things. No relative or friend was with him. It was very sad. I was with him considerable, only just sitting by him soothing him. He was wandering all the time. His talk was so affecting it kept the tears in my eyes much of the time. The last twenty-four hours he sank very rapidly. He had been sick some months ago and was put in the 6th Invalid Corps — they ought to have sent him home instead. The next morning after his death his brother came, a very fine man, postmaster at Lyne Ridge, Pa. — he was much affected, and well he might be.

Mother, I think it worse than ever here in the hospitals. We are getting the dregs as it were of the sickness and awful hardships of the past three years. There is the most horrible cases of diarrhœa you ever conceived of, and by the hundreds and thousands; I suppose from such

Letters of 1864

diet as they have in the army. Well, dear mother, I will not write any more on the sick, and yet I know you wish to hear about them. Every one is so unfeeling; it has got to be an old story. There is no good nursing. O I wish you were — or rather women of such qualities as you and Mat — were here in plenty, to be stationed as matrons among the poor sick and wounded men. Just to be present would be enough — O what good it would do them. Mother, I feel so sick when I see what kind of people there are among them, with charge over them — so cold and ceremonious, afraid to touch them. Well, mother, I fear I have written you a flighty kind of a letter — I write in haste. WALT. .

The papers came right, mother — love to Jeff, Mat, and all.

VII

Washington, March 22, 1864. DEAREST MOTHER — I feel quite bad to hear that you are not well — have a pain in your side, and a very bad cold. Dear mother, I hope it is better. I wish you would write to me, or Jeff would, right away, as I shall not feel easy until I hear. I rec'd George's letter. Jeff wrote with it, about your feeling pretty sick, and the pain. Mother, I also rec'd your letter a few days before. You say the Browns acted very mean, and I should say they

The Wound Dresser

did indeed, but as it is going to remain the same about the house, I should let it all pass. I am very glad Mat and Jeff are going to remain; I should not have felt satisfied if they and you had been separated. I have written a letter to Han, with others enclosed, a good long letter (took two postage stamps). I have written to George too, directed it to Knoxville. Mother, everything is the same with me; I am feeling very well indeed, the old trouble of my head stopt and my ears affected, has not troubled me any since I came back here from Brooklyn. I am writing this in Major Hapgood's old office, cor. 15th and F streets, where I have my old table and window. It is dusty and chilly to-day, anything but agreeable. Gen. Grant is expected every moment now in the Army of the Potomac to take active command. I have just this moment heard from the front—there is nothing yet of a movement, but each side is continually on the alert, expecting something to happen. O mother, to think that we are to have here soon what I have seen so many times, the awful loads and trains and boat loads of poor bloody and pale and wounded young men again — for that is what we certainly will, and before very long. I see all the little signs, geting ready in the hospitals, etc.; it is dreadful when one thinks about it. I sometimes think over the sights I have myself seen, the arrival of the wounded after a battle, and the scenes on the field too, and I can hardly believe my own recollections. What an awful thing war is! Mother, it seems not

Letters of 1864

men but a lot of devils and butchers butchering each other.

Dear mother, I think twenty times a day about your sickness. O, I hope it is not so bad as Jeff wrote. He said you was worse than you had ever been before, and he would write me again. Well, he must, even if only a few lines. What have you heard from Mary and her family, anything? Well, dear mother, I hope this will find you quite well of the pain, and of the cold — write about the little girls and Mat and all. WALT.

VIII

Washington, March 29, 1864. DEAREST MOTHER — I have written to George again to Knoxville. Things seem to be quiet down there so far. We think here that our forces are going to be made strongest here in Virginia this spring, and every thing bent to take Richmond. Grant is here; he is now down at headquarters in the field, Brandy station. We expect fighting before long; there are many indications. I believe I told you they had sent up all the sick from front. [*The letter is here mutilated so as to be illegible; from the few remaining words, however, it is possible to gather that the writer is describing the arrival of a* train of wounded, over 600, *in Washington during* a terribly rainy afternoon. *The letter continues:*] I could not keep the tears out of my eyes. Many of the poor young men had to be moved on

The Wound Dresser

stretchers, with blankets over them, which soon soaked as wet as water in the rain. Most were sick cases, but some badly wounded. I came up to the nearest hospital and helped. Mother, it was a dreadful night (last Friday night) — pretty dark, the wind gusty, and the rain fell in torrents. One poor boy — this is a sample of one case out of the 600 — he seemed to be quite young, he was quite small (I looked at his body afterwards), he groaned some as the stretcher bearers were carrying him along, and again as they carried him through the hospital gate. They set down the stretcher and examined him, and the poor boy was dead. They took him into the ward, and the doctor came immediately, but it was all of no use. The worst of it is, too, that he is entirely unknown — there was nothing on his clothes, or any one with him to identify him, and he is altogether unknown. Mother, it is enough to rack one's heart — such things. Very likely his folks will never know in the world what has become of him. Poor, poor child, for he appeared as though he could be but 18. I feel lately as though I must have some intermission. I feel well and hearty enough, and was never better, but my feelings are kept in a painful condition a great part of the time. Things get worse and worse, as to the amount and sufferings of the sick, and as I have said before, those who have to do with them are getting more and more callous and indifferent. Mother, when I see the common soldiers, what they go through, and how everybody seems to try to

Letters of 1864

pick upon them, and what humbug there is over them every how, even the dying soldier's money stolen from his body by some scoundrel attendant, or from [the] sick one, even from under his head, which is a common thing, and then the agony I see every day, I get almost frightened at the world. Mother, I will try to write more cheerfully next time — but I see so much. Well, goodbye for present, dear mother. WALT.

IX

Washington, Thursday afternoon, March 31, 1864.
DEAREST MOTHER — I have just this moment received your letter dated last Monday evening. Dear mother, I have not seen anything in any paper where the 51st is, nor heard anything, but I do not feel any ways uneasy about them. I presume they are at Knoxville, Tennessee. Mother, they are now paying off many of the regiments in this army — but about George, I suppose there will be delays in sending money, etc. Dear mother, I wish I had some money to send you, but I am living very close by the wind. Mother, I will try somehow to send you something worth while, and I do hope you will not worry and feel unhappy about money matters; I know things are very high. Mother, I suppose you got my letter written Tuesday last, 29th March, did you not? I have been going to write to Jeff for more than a month — I laid out to write a good long letter,

The Wound Dresser

but something has prevented me, one thing and another; but I will try to write to-morrow sure. Mother, I have been in the midst of suffering and death for two months worse than ever — the only comfort is that I have been the cause of some beams of sunshine upon their suffering and gloomy souls, and bodies too. Many of the dying I have been with, too.

Well, mother, you must not worry about the grocery bill, etc., though I suppose you will say that it is easier said than followed (as to me, I believe I worry about worldly things less than ever, if that is possible). Tell Jeff and Mat I send them my love. Gen. Grant has just come in town from front. The country here is all mad again. I am going to a spiritualist medium this evening — I expect it will be a humbug, of course. I will tell you next letter. Dear mother, keep a good heart. WALT.

How is California? Tell Hat her Uncle Walt will come home one of these days, and take her to New York to walk in Broadway. Poor little Jim, I should like to see him. There is a rich young friend of mine wants me to go to Idaho with him to make money.

X

Washington, Tuesday afternoon, April 5, 1864.
DEAREST MOTHER — I got a letter from Jeff yesterday — he says you often work too hard, exposing yourself, I suppose, scrubbing, etc., and

Letters of 1864

the worst of it is I am afraid it is true. Mother, I would take things easy, and let up on the scrubbing and such things; they may be needed perhaps, but they ain't half as much needed as that you should be as well as possible, and free from rheumatism and cold. Jeff says that —— has had the chicken pox. Has she got all over it? I want to hear. So Nance has had another child, poor little one; there don't seem to be much show for it, poor little young one, these times. We are having awful rainy weather here. It is raining to-day steady and spiteful enough. The soldiers in camp are having the benefit of it, and the sick, many of them. There is a great deal of rheumatism and also throat disease, and they are affected by the weather. I have writ to George again, directed to Knoxville. Mother, I got a letter this morning from Lewis Brown, the young man that had his leg amputated two months or so ago (the one that I slept in the hospital by several nights for fear of hemorrhage from the amputation). He is home at Elkton, Maryland, on furlough. He wants me to come out there, but I believe I shall not go — he is doing very well. There are many very bad now in hospital, so many of the soldiers are getting broke down after two years, or two and a half, exposure and bad diet, pork, hard biscuit, bad water or none at all, etc., etc. — so we have them brought up here. Oh, it is terrible, and getting worse, worse, worse. I thought it was bad; to see these I sometimes think is more pitiful still.

The Wound Dresser

Well, mother, I went to see the great spirit medium, Foster. There were some little things some might call curious, perhaps, but it is a shallow thing and a humbug. A gentleman who was with me was somewhat impressed, but I could not see anything in it worth calling supernatural. I would n't turn on my heel to go again and see such things, or twice as much. We had table rappings and lots of nonsense. I will give you particulars when I come home one of these days. Jeff, I believe there is a fate on your long letter; I thought I would write it to-day, but as it happens I will hardly get this in the mail, I fear, in time for to-day. O how I want to see you all, and Sis and Hat. Well, I have scratched out a great letter just as fast as I could write.

Wednesday forenoon. Mother, I did n't get the letter in the mail yesterday. I have just had my breakfast, some good tea and good toast and butter. I write this in my room, 456 Sixth st. The storm seems to be over. Dear mother, I hope you are well and in good spirits — write to me often as you can, and Jeff too. Any news from Han? WALT.

XI

Washington, April 10, 1864. DEAREST MOTHER — I rec'd your letter and sent the one you sent for George immediately — he must have got it the next day. I had got one from

Letters of 1864

him before yours arrived. I mean to go to Annapolis and see him.

Mother, we expect a commencement of the fighting below very soon; there is every indication of it. We have had about as severe rain storms here lately as I ever see. It is middling pleasant now. There are exciting times in Congress — the Copperheads are getting furious and want to recognize the Southern Confederacy. This is a pretty time to talk of recognizing such villains after what they have done, and after what has transpired the last three years. After first Fredericksburg I felt discouraged myself, and doubted whether our rulers could carry on the war — but that has passed away. The war must be carried on, and I could willingly go myself in the ranks if I thought it would profit more than at present, and I don't know sometimes but I shall as it is. Mother, you don't know what a feeling a man gets after being in the active sights and influences of the camp, the army, the wounded, etc. He gets to have a deep feeling he never experienced before — the flag, the tune of Yankee Doodle and similar things, produce an effect on a fellow never such before. I have seen some bring tears on the men's cheeks, and others turn pale, under such circumstances. I have a little flag; it belonged to one of our cavalry reg'ts; presented to me by one of the wounded. It was taken by the Secesh in a cavalry fight, and rescued by our men in a bloody little skirmish. It cost three men's lives, just to get one

The Wound Dresser

little flag, four by three. Our men rescued it, and tore it from the breast of a dead Rebel — all that just for the name of getting their little banner back again. The man that got it was very badly wounded, and they let him keep it. I was with him a good deal; he wanted to give me something, he said, he did n't expect to live, so he gave me the little banner as a keepsake. I mention this, mother, to show you a specimen of the feeling. There is n't a reg't, cavalry or infantry, that would n't do the same on occasion.

Tuesday morning, April 12. Mother, I will finish my letter this morning. It is a beautiful day to-day. I was up in Congress very late last night. The house had a very excited night session about expelling the men that want to recognize the Southern Confederacy. You ought to hear the soldiers talk. They are excited to madness. We shall probably have hot times here, not in the army alone. The soldiers are true as the North Star. I send you a couple of envelopes, and one to George. Write how you are, dear mother, and all the rest. I want to see you all. Jeff, my dear brother, I wish you was here, and Mat too. Write how Sis is. I am well, as usual; indeed first rate every way. I want to come on in a month and try to print my " Drum-Taps." I think it may be a success pecuniarily, too. Dearest mother, I hope this will find you entirely well, and dear sister Mat and all. WALT.

Letters of 1864

XII

Washington, Tuesday noon, April 19, 1864. DEAREST MOTHER — I haven't heard any news from home now in more than a week. I hope you are well, dear mother, and all the rest too. There is nothing new with me. I can only write the same old story about going to the hospitals, etc., etc. I have not heard anything since from George — have you heard anything further? I have written to him to Annapolis. We are having it pretty warm here to-day, after a long spell of rain storms, but the last two or three days very fine. Mother, I suppose you got my letter of last Tuesday, 12th. I went down to the Capitol the nights of the debate on the expulsion of Mr. Long last week. They had night sessions, very late. I like to go to the House of Representatives at night; it is the most magnificent hall, so rich and large, and lighter at night than it is days, and still not a light visible — it comes through the glass roof — but the speaking and the ability of the members is nearly always on a low scale. It is very curious and melancholy to see such a rate of talent there, such tremendous times as these — I should say about the same range of genius as our old friend Dr. Swaim, just about. You may think I am joking, but I am not, mother — I am speaking in perfect earnest. The Capitol grows upon one in time, especially as they have got the great figure on top of it now, and you can see it very

The Wound Dresser

well. It is a great bronze figure, the Genius of Liberty I suppose. It looks wonderful towards sundown. I love to go and look at it. The sun when it is nearly down shines on the headpiece and it dazzles and glistens like a big star; it looks quite curious.

Well, mother, we have commenced on another summer, and what it will bring forth who can tell? The campaign of this summer is expected here to be more active and severe than any yet. As I told you in a former letter, Grant is determined to bend everything to take Richmond and break up the banditti of scoundrels that have stuck themselves up there as a " government." He is in earnest about it; his whole soul and all his thoughts night and day are upon it. He is probably the most in earnest of any man in command or in the Government either—that's something, ain't it, mother?—and they are bending everything to fight for their last chance—calling in their forces from Southwest, etc. Dear mother, give my love to dear brother Jeff and Mat and all. I write this in my room, 6th st.

WALT.

XIII

Washington, April 26, 1864. DEAREST MOTHER — Burnside's army passed through here yesterday. I saw George and walked with him in the regiment for some distance and had quite a talk. He is very well; he is very much tanned and looks

Letters of 1864

hardy. I told him all the latest news from home. George stands it very well, and looks and behaves the same noble and good fellow he always was and always will be. It was on 14th st. I watched three hours before the 51st came along. I joined him just before they came to where the President and Gen. Burnside were standing with others on a balcony, and the interest of seeing me, etc., made George forget to notice the President and salute him. He was a little annoyed at forgetting it. I called his attention to it, but we had passed a little too far on, and George would n't turn round even ever so little. However, there was a great many more than half the army passed without noticing Mr. Lincoln and the others, for there was a great crowd all through the streets, especially here, and the place where the President stood was not conspicuous from the rest. The 9th Corps made a very fine show indeed. There were, I should think, five very full regiments of new black troops, under Gen. Ferrero. They looked and marched very well. It looked funny to see the President standing with his hat off to them just the same as the rest as they passed by. Then there [were the] Michigan regiments; one of them was a regiment of sharpshooters, partly composed of Indians. Then there was a pretty strong force of artillery and a middling force of cavalry — many New York, Pennsylvania, Massachusetts, R.I., etc., reg'ts. All except the blacks were veterans [that had] seen plenty of fighting. Mother, it is very different to see a real army of fighting men, from

The Wound Dresser

one of those shows in Brooklyn, or New York, or on Fort Greene. Mother, it was a curious sight to see these ranks after rank of our own dearest blood of men, mostly young, march by, worn and sunburnt and sweaty, with well-worn clothes and thin bundles, and knapsacks, tin cups, and some with frying pans strapt over their backs, all dirty and sweaty, nothing real neat about them except their muskets; but they were all as clean and bright as silver. They were four or five hours passing along, marching with wide ranks pretty quickly, too. It is a great sight to see an army 25 or 30,000 on the march. They are all so gay, too. Poor fellows, nothing dampens their spirits. They all got soaked with rain the night before. I saw Fred McReady and Capt. Sims, and Col. Le Gendre, etc. I don't know exactly where Burnside's army is going. Among other rumors it is said they [are] to go [with] the Army of the Potomac to act as a reserve force, etc. Another is that they are to make a flank march, to go round and get Lee on the side, etc. I haven't been out this morning and don't know what news — we know nothing, only that there is without doubt to be a terrible campaign here in Virginia this summer, and that all who know deepest about it are very serious about it. Mother, it is serious times. I do not feel to fret or whimper, but in my heart and soul about our country, the forthcoming campaign with all its vicissitudes and the wounded and slain — I dare say, mother, I feel the reality more than some

Letters of 1864

because I am in the midst of its saddest results so much. Others may say what they like, I believe in Grant and in Lincoln, too. I think Grant deserves to be trusted. He is working continually. No one knows his plans; we will only know them when he puts them in operation. Our army is very large here in Virginia this spring, and they are still pouring in from east and west. You don't see about it in the papers, but we have a very large army here.

Mother, I am first rate in health, thank God; I never was better. Dear mother, have you got over all that distress and sickness in your head? You must write particular about it. Dear brother Jeff, how are you, and how is Matty, and how the dear little girls? Jeff, I believe the devil is in it about my writing you; I have laid out so many weeks to write you a good long letter, and something has shoved it off each time. Never mind, mother's letters keep you posted. You must write, and don't forget to tell me all about Sis. Is she as good and interesting as she was six months ago? Mother, have you heard anything from Han? Mother, I have just had my breakfast. I had it in my room — some hard biscuit warmed on the stove, and a bowl of strong tea with good milk and sugar. I have given a Michigan soldier his breakfast with me. He relished it, too; he has just gone. Mother, I have just heard again that Burnside's troops are to be a reserve to protect Washington, so there may be something in it. WALT.

The Wound Dresser

It is very fine weather here yesterday and to-day. The hospitals are very full; they are putting up hundreds of hospital tents.

XIV

Washington, April 28, 1864. DEAREST MOTHER — I thought I would write you just a line, though I have nothing of importance — only the talk of the street here seems more and more to assert that Burnside's army is to remain near here to protect Washington and act as a reserve, so that Grant can move the Army of the Potomac upon Richmond, without being compelled to turn and be anxious about the Capital; also that Burnside can attend to Lee if the latter should send any force up west of here (what they call the valley of the Shenandoah), or invade Pennsylvania again. I thought you would like to hear this; it looks plausible, but there are lots of rumors of all kinds. I cannot hear where Burnside's army is, as they don't allow the papers to print army movements, but I fancy they are very near Washington, the other side of Arlington heights, this moment. Mother, I wrote yesterday to Han, and sent one of George's letters from Annapolis. Mother, I suppose you got my letter of Tuesday, 26th. I have not heard anything from you in quite a little while. I am still well. The weather is fine; quite hot yesterday. Mother, I am now going down to see a poor soldier who is very low

Letters of 1864

with a long diarrhœa — he cannot recover. When I was with him last night, he asked me before I went away to ask God's blessing on him. He says, I am no scholar and you are — poor dying man, I told him I hoped from the bottom of my heart God would bless him, and bring him up yet. I soothed him as well as I could; it was affecting, I can tell you. Jeff, I wrote to Mr. Kirkwood yesterday to 44 Pierrepont st. He sent me some money last Monday. Is Probasco still in the store in N. Y.? Dear sister Mat, I quite want to see you and California, not forgetting my little Hattie, too. WALT.

2 o'clock, 28th April. DEAREST MOTHER — Just as I was going to mail this I received authentic information [that] Burnside's army is now about 16 or 18 miles south of here, at a place called Fairfax Court House. They had last night no orders to move at present, and I rather think they will remain there, or near there. What I have written before as a rumor about their being to be held as a reserve, to act whenever occasion may need them, is now quite decided on. You may hear a rumor in New York that they have been shipped in transports from Alexandria — there is no truth in it at all. Grant's Army of the Potomac is probably to do the heavy work. His army is strong and full of fight. Mother, I think it is to-day the noblest army of soldiers that ever marched — nobody can know the men as well as I do, I sometimes think.

Mother, I am writing this in Willard's hotel,

The Wound Dresser

on my way down to hospital after I leave this at post office. I shall come out to dinner at 4 o'clock and then go back to hospital again in evening.

Good bye, dear mother and all. WALT.

XV

Washington, May 3, 1864. DEAREST MOTHER —I received your letter dated last Friday afternoon, with one from Mr. Heyde. It seems by that Han is better, but, as you say, it would be much more satisfactory if Han would write to us herself. Mother, I believe I told you I sent a letter to Han last week, enclosing one of George's from Annapolis. I was glad to get Heyde's letter, though, as it was. Mother, I am sorry you still have returns of your cold. Does it affect your head like it did? Dear mother, I hope you will not expose yourself, nor work too much, but take things easier. I have nothing different to write about the war, or movements here. What I wrote last Thursday, about Burnside's Corps being probably used as a reserve, is still talked of here, and seems to be probable. A large force is necessary to guard the railroad between here and Culpepper, and also to keep from any emergency that might happen, and I should n't wonder if the 9th would be used for such purpose, at least for the present. I think the 51st must be down

Letters of 1864

not very far from Fairfax Court House yet, but I haven't heard certain.

Mother, I have seen a person up from front this morning. There is no movement yet and no fighting started. The men are in their camps yet. Gen. Grant is at Culpepper. You need not pay the slightest attention to such things as you mention in the *Eagle*, about the 9th Corps — the writer of it, and very many of the writers on war matters in those papers, don't know one bit more on what they are writing about than Ed does. Mother, you say in your letter you got my letter the previous afternoon. Why, mother, you ought to [have] got it Wednesday forenoon, or afternoon at furthest. This letter now will get in New York Wednesday morning, by daylight — you ought to get it before noon. The postmaster in Brooklyn must have a pretty set of carriers, to take twice as long to take a letter from New York to you as it does to go from Washington to N. Y. Mother, I suppose you got a letter from me Friday, also, as I wrote a second letter on Thursday last, telling you the 9th Corps was camped then about sixteen miles from here.

About George's pictures, perhaps you better wait till I hear from him, before sending them. I remain well as usual. The poor fellow I mentioned in one of my letters last week, with diarrhœa, that wanted me to ask God's blessing on him, was still living yesterday afternoon, but just living. He is only partially conscious, is all wasted away to nothing, and lies most of the time

The Wound Dresser

in half stupor, as they give him brandy copiously. Yesterday I was there by him a few minutes. He is very much averse to taking brandy, and there was some trouble in getting him to take it. He is almost totally deaf the last five or six days. There is no chance for him at all. Quite a particular friend of mine, Oscar Cunningham, an Ohio boy, had his leg amputated yesterday close up by the thigh. It was a pretty tough operation. He was badly wounded just a year ago to-day at Chancellorsville and has suffered a great deal; lately got erysipelas in his leg and foot. I forget whether I have mentioned him before or not. He was a very large, noble-looking young man when I first see him. The doctor thinks he will live and get up, but I consider [it] by no means so certain. He is very much prostrated. Well, dear mother, you must write and Jeff too — I do want to see you all very much. How does Mat get along, and how little Sis and all? I send my love to you and Jeff and all. We are having a very pleasant, coolish day here. I am going down to post office to leave this, and then up to my old friends the O'Connors to dinner, and then down to hospital. Well, good-bye, dear mother, for present. WALT.

Tuesday afternoon, 3 o'clock. Mother, just as I was going to seal my letter, Major Hapgood has come in from the P. O. and brings me a few lines from George, which I enclose — you will see they were written four days ago.

Letters of 1864

XVI

Washington, May 6, 1864. DEAREST MOTHER — I write you a few lines, as I know you feel anxious these times. I suppose the New York papers must have it in this morning that the Army of the Potomac has made a move, and has crossed the Rapidan river. At any rate that is the case. As near as I can learn about Burnside's army, that lies in the rear of the Army of the Potomac (from Warrenton, Virginia and so to Rappahannock river and up toward Manassas). It still appears to be kept as a reserve and for emergencies, etc. I have not heard anything from the 51st. Mother, of course you got my letter of Tuesday, 3rd, with the letter from George dated Bristoe station. I have writ to George since, and addressed the letter Warrenton, Va., or elsewhere, thinking he might get it.

Mother, the idea is entertained quite largely here that the Rebel army will retreat to Richmond, as it is well known that Grant is very strong (most folks say too strong for Lee). I suppose you know we menace them almost as much from up Fortress Monroe as we do from the Rapidan. Butler and W. F. Smith are down there with at least fifty or sixty thousand men, and will move up simultaneously with Grant. The occasion is very serious, and anxious, but somehow I am full of hope, and feel that we shall take Richmond — (I hope to go there yet before the hot weather is

The Wound Dresser

past). Dear mother, I hope you are well, and little California — love to Jeff and Mat and all.
WALT.

Mother, you ought to get this letter Saturday forenoon, as it will be in N. Y. by sunrise Saturday, 7th.

Mother, the poor soldier with diarrhœa is still living, but, O, what a looking object; death would be a boon to him; he cannot last many hours. Cunningham, the Ohio boy with leg amputated at thigh, has picked up beyond expectation now! — looks altogether like getting well. The hospitals are very full. I am very well indeed — pretty warm here to-day

XVII

Washington, Monday, 2 o'clock — May 9, '64.
DEAREST MOTHER — There is nothing from the army more than you know in the N. Y. papers. The fighting has been hard enough, but the papers make lots of additional items, and a good deal that they just entirely make up. There are from 600 to 1000 wounded coming up here — not 6 to 8000 as the papers have it. I cannot hear what part the 9th Corps took in the fight of Friday and afterwards, nor whether they really took any at all — (they, the papers, are determined to make up just anything). Mother, I received your letter and Han's — and was glad indeed to get both.

Letters of 1864

Mother, you must not be under such apprehension, as I think it is not warranted.

So far as we get news here, we are gaining the day, so far *decidedly*. If the news we hear is true that Lee has been repulsed and driven back by Grant, and that we are masters of the field, and pursuing them — then I think Lee will retreat south, and Richmond will be abandoned by the Rebs. But of course time only can develope what will happen. Mother, I will write again Wednesday, or before, if I hear anything to write. Love to Jeff and Mat and all. WALT.

XVIII

Washington, May 10, '64 (½ past 2 p. m.) DEAREST MOTHER — There is nothing perhaps more than you see in the N. Y. papers. The fighting down in the field on the 6th I think ended in our favor, though with pretty severe losses to some of our divisions. The fighting is about 70 miles from here, and 50 from Richmond — on the 7th and 8th followed up by the Rebel army hauling off, they say retreating, and Meade pursuing. It is quite mixed yet, but I guess we have the best of it. If we really have, Richmond is a goner, for they cannot do any better than they have done. The 9th Corps was in the fight, and where I cannot tell yet, but from the wounded I have seen I don't think that Corps was deeply in.

The Wound Dresser

I have seen 300 wounded. They came in last night. I asked for men of 9th Corps, but could not find any at all. These 300 men were not badly wounded, mostly in arms, hands, trunk of body, etc. They could all walk, though some had an awful time of it. They had to fight their way with the worst in the middle out of the region of Fredericksburg, and so on where they could get across the Rappahannock and get where they found transportation to Washington. The Gov't has decided, (or rather Gen. Meade has) to occupy Fredericksburg for depot and hospital — (I think that is a first rate decision) — so the wounded men will receive quick attention and surgery, instead of being racked through the long journey up here. Still, many come in here. Mother, my impression is that we have no great reason for alarm or sadness about George so far. Of course I *know* nothing. Well, good-bye, dearest mother. WALT.

Mother, I wrote you yesterday, too. Tell dear brother Jeff to write me. Love to Mat. The poor diarrhœa man died, and it was a boon. Oscar Cunningham, 82nd Ohio, has had a relapse. I fear it is going bad with him. Lung diseases are quite plenty — night before last I staid in hospital all night tending a poor fellow. It has been awful hot here — milder to-day.

Letters of 1864

XIX

[*Washington*] *May 12, ½ past 5 p. m.* DEAREST MOTHER — George is all right, unhurt, up to Tuesday morning, 10th inst. The 51st was in a bad battle last Friday; lost 20 killed, between 40 and 50 wounded. I have just seen some of the 51st wounded just arrived, one of them Fred Saunders, Corporal Co. K, George's company. He said when he left the 51st was in rear on guard duty. He left Tuesday morning last. The papers have it that Burnside's Corps was in a fight Tuesday, but I think it most probable the 51st was not in it.

Fred McReady is wounded badly, but not seriously. Sims is safe. You see Le Gendre is wounded — he was shot through the bridge of nose.

Mother, you ought to get this Friday forenoon, 13th. I will write again soon. Wrote once before to-day. WALT.

The Wound Dresser

XX

Washington, May 13, 1864, 2 o'clock p. m. DEAREST MOTHER — I wrote you a hurried letter late yesterday afternoon but left it myself at the P. O. in time for the mail. You ought to have got it this forenoon, or afternoon at furthest. I sent you two letters yesterday. I hope the carrier brings you your letters the same day. I wrote to the Brooklyn postmaster about it. I have heard from George up to Tuesday morning last, 10th, till which time he was safe. The battle of Friday, 6th, was very severe. George's Co. K lost one acting sergeant, Sturgis, killed, 2 men killed, 4 wounded. As I wrote yesterday, I have seen here Corp. Fred Saunders of Co. K, who was wounded in side, nothing serious, in Friday's fight, and came up here. I also talked with Serg. Brown, Co. F, 51st, rather badly wounded in right shoulder. Saunders said, when he left Tuesday morning he heard (or saw them there, I forget which) the 51st and its whole division were on guard duty toward the rear. The 9th Corps, however, has had hard fighting since, but whether the division or brigade the 51st is in was in the fights of Tuesday, 10th, (a pretty severe one) or Wednesday, I cannot tell, and it is useless to make calculations — and the only way is to wait and hope for the best. As I wrote yesterday, there were some 30 of 51st reg't killed and 50 wounded in Friday's battle, 6th inst. I have seen Col. Le Gendre. He is here in Washington not far from

Letters of 1864

where I am, 485 12th st. is his address. Poor man, I felt sorry indeed for him. He is badly wounded and disfigured. He is shot through the bridge of the nose, and left eye probably lost. I spent a little time with him this forenoon. He is suffering very much, spoke of George very kindly; said " Your brother is well." His orderly told me he saw him, George, Sunday night last, well. Fred McReady is wounded in hip, I believe bone fractured — bad enough, but not deeply serious. I cannot hear of his arrival here. If he comes I shall find him immediately and take care of him myself. He is probably yet at Fredericksburg, but will come up, I think. Yesterday and to-day the badly wounded are coming in. The long lists of *previous arrivals*, (I suppose they are all reprinted at great length in N. Y. papers) are of men three-fourths of them quite slightly wounded, and the rest hurt pretty bad. I was thinking, mother, if one could see the men who arrived in the first squads, of two or three hundred at a time, one would n't be alarmed at those terrible long lists. Still there is a sufficient sprinkling of deeply distressing cases. I find my hands full all the time, with new and old cases — poor suffering young men, I think of them, and do try, mother, to do what I can for them, (and not think of the vexatious skedaddlers and merely scratched ones, of whom there are too many lately come here).

Dearest mother, I hope you and all are well — you must keep a good heart. Still, the fighting

The Wound Dresser

is very mixed, but it *seems steadily turning into real successes* for Grant. The news to-day here is very good — you will see it [in the] N. Y. papers. I steadily believe Grant is going to succeed, and that we shall have Richmond — but O what a price to pay for it. We have had a good rain here and it is pleasanter and cooler. I shall write very soon again. WALT.

XXI

Washington, May 18, 1864. DEAREST MOTHER — I will only write you a hasty note this time, as I am pretty tired, and my head feels disagreeable from being in too much. I was up yesterday to Carver hospital and again saw the man of the 51st, Thos. McCowell, who told me of George, up to latter part of Thursday, 12th inst. I questioned him, and his story was very clear, so I felt perfectly satisfied. He is wounded in hand; will be transferred soon to New York and may call on you. He is a young Irishman, and seems to be a very good fellow indeed. I have written to George, day before yesterday. Did you send my last letter to Han? If not, send it yet. Mother, I see such awful things. I expect one of these days, if I live, I shall have awful thoughts and dreams — but it is such a great thing to be able to do some real good; assuage these horri-

Letters of 1864

ble pains and wounds, and save life even — that's the only thing that keeps a fellow up.

Well, dear mother, I make such reckoning of yet coming on and seeing you. How I want to see Jeff, too — O, it is too bad I have not written to him so long — and Mat, too, and little California and all. I am going out now a little while. I remain first rate, as well as ever. WALT

XXII

Washington, Monday forenoon, May 23, '64.
DEAR BROTHER JEFF—I received your letter yesterday. I too had got a few lines from George, dated on the field, 16th. He said he had also just written to mother. I cannot make out there has been any fighting since in which the 9th Corps has been engaged. I do hope mother will not get despondent and so unhappy. I suppose it is idle to say I think George's chances are very good for coming out of this campaign safe, yet at present it seems to me so — but it is indeed idle to say so, for no one can tell what a day may bring forth. Sometimes I think that should it come, when it *must* be, to fall in battle, one's anguish over a son or brother killed would be tempered with much to take the edge off. I can honestly say it has no terrors for me, if I had to be hit in battle, as far as I myself am concerned. It would be a

The Wound Dresser

noble and manly death and in the best cause. Then one finds, as I have the past year, that our feelings and imaginations make a thousand times too much of the whole matter. Of the many I have seen die, or known of, the past year, I have not seen or heard of *one* who met death with any terror. Yesterday afternoon I spent a good part of the afternoon with a young man of 17, named Charles Cutter, of Lawrence city, Mass., 1st Mass. heavy artillery, battery M. He was brought in to one of the hospitals mortally wounded in abdomen. Well, I thought to myself as I sat looking at him, it ought to be a relief to his folks after all, if they could see how little he suffered. He lay very placid in a half lethargy with his eyes closed. It was very warm, and I sat a long while fanning him and wiping the sweat. At length he opened his eyes quite wide and clear and looked inquiringly around. I said, "What is it, my dear? do you want anything?" He said quietly, with a good natured smile, "O nothing; I was only looking around to see who was with me." His mind was somewhat wandering, yet he lay so peaceful, in his dying condition. He seemed to be a real New England country boy, so good natured, with a pleasant homely way, and quite a fine looking boy. Without any doubt he died in course of night.

There don't seem to be any war news of importance very late. We have been fearfully disappointed with Sigel not making his junction from the lower part of the valley, and perhaps harassing

Letters of 1864

Lee's left or left rear, which the junction or equivalent to it was an indispensable part of Grant's plan, we think. This is one great reason why things have lagged so with the Army. Some here are furious with Sigel. You will see he has been superseded. His losses [in] his repulse are not so important, though annoying enough, but it was of the greatest consequence that he should have hastened through the gaps ten or twelve days ago at all hazards and come in from the west, keeping near enough to our right to have assistance if he needed it. Jeff, I suppose you know that there has been quite a large army lying idle, mostly of artillery reg'ts, manning the numerous forts around here. They have been the fattest and heartiest reg'ts anywhere to be seen, and full in numbers, some of them numbering 2000 men. Well, they have all, every one, been shoved down to the front. Lately we have had the militia reg'ts pouring in here, mostly from Ohio. They look first rate. I saw two or three come in yesterday, splendid American young men, from farms mostly. We are to have them for a hundred days and probably they will not refuse to stay another hundred. Jeff, tell mother I shall write Wednesday certain (or if I hear anything I will write to-morrow). I still think we shall get Richmond. WALT.

Jeff, you must take this up to mother as soon as you go home. Jeff, I have changed my quarters. I moved Saturday last. I am now at 502 Pennsylvania av., near 3rd st. I still go a little

The Wound Dresser

almost daily to Major Hapgood's, cor. 15th and F sts., 5th floor. Am apt to be there about 12 or 1. See Fred McReady and others of 51st. George's letter to me of 16th I sent to Han. Should like to see Mr. Worther if he comes here — give my best remembrance to Mr. Lane.

I may very likely go down for a few days to Ball Plain and Fredericksburg, but one is wanted here permanently more than any other place. I have written to George several times in hopes one at least may reach him. Matty, my dear sister, how are you getting along? O how I should like to see you this very day.

XXIII

Washington, May 25, 1864. DEAREST MOTHER — I have not heard anything of George or the reg't or Corps more than I have already written. I got Jeff's letter on Sunday and wrote to him next day, which you have seen, mother, of course. I have written to Han and sent her George's letter to me dated 16th. I have heard that the 9th Corps has been moved to the extreme left of the army. I should think by accounts this morning that the army must be nearly half way from Fredericksburg to Richmond. The advance can't be more than 30 to 35 miles from there. I see Fred McReady about every other

Letters of 1864

day. I have to go down to Alexandria, about 6 miles from here. He is doing quite well, but very tired of the confinement. I still go around daily and nightly among wounded. Mother, it is just the same old story; poor suffering young men, great swarms of them, come up here now every day all battered and bloody — there have 4000 arrived here this morning, and 1500 yesterday. They appear to be bringing them all up here from Fredericksburg. The journey from the field till they get aboard the boats at Ball plain is horrible. I believe I wrote several times about Oscar Cunningham, 82nd Ohio, amputation of right leg, wounded over a year ago, a friend of mine here. He is rapidly sinking; said to me yesterday, O, if he could only die. The young lad Cutter, of 1st Massachusetts heavy artillery, I was with Sunday afternoon, (I wrote about in Jeff's letter) still holds out. Poor boy, there is no chance for him at all.

But mother, I shall make you gloomy enough if I go on with these kind of particulars — only I know you like to hear about the poor young men, after I have once begun to mention them. Mother, I have changed my quarters — am at 502 Pennsylvania av., near 3d street, only a little way from the Capitol. Where I was, the house was sold and the old lady I hired the room from had to move out and give the owner possession. I like my new quarters pretty well — I have a room to myself, 3d story hall bedroom. I have my meals in the house. Mother, it must be sad

The Wound Dresser

enough about Nance and the young ones. Is the little baby still hearty? I believe you wrote a few weeks after it was born that it was quite a fine child. I see you had a draft in the 3d Congressional district. I was glad enough to see Jeff's name was not drawn. We have had it awful hot here, but there was a sharp storm of thunder and lightning last night, and to-day it is fine. Mother, do any of the soldiers I see here from Brooklyn or New York ever call upon you? They sometimes say they will here. Tell Jeff I got a letter yesterday from W. E. Worthen, in which he sent me some money for the men. I have acknowledged it to Mr. W. by letter. Well, dear mother, I must close. O, how I want to see you all — I will surely have to come home as soon as this Richmond campaign is decided — then I want to print my new book. Love to Mat — write to a fellow often as you can. WALT.

XXIV

Washington, May 30, 1864. DEAREST MOTHER — I have no news at all to write this time. I have not heard anything of the 51st since I last wrote you, and about the general war news only what you see in the papers. Grant is gradually getting nearer and nearer to Richmond. Many here anticipate that should Grant go into Richmond,

Letters of 1864

Lee will make a side movement and march up west into the North, either to attempt to strike Washington, or to go again into Pennsylvania. I only say if that should happen, I for one shall not be dissatisfied so very much. Well, mother, how are you getting along home? — how do you feel in health these days, dear mother? I hope you are well and in good heart yet. I remain pretty well: my head begins to trouble me a little with a sort of fullness, as it often does in the hot weather. Singular to relate, the 1st Mass. artillery boy, Charles Cutter, is still living, and may get well. I saw him this morning. I am still around among wounded same, but will not make you feel blue by filling my letter with sad particulars.

I am writing this in Willard's hotel, hurrying to catch this afternoon's mail. Mother, do you get your letters now next morning, as you ought? I got a letter from the postmaster of Brooklyn about it — said if the letters were neglected again, to send him word. I have not heard from home now in some days. I am going to put up a lot of my old things in a box and send them home by express. I will write when I send them. Have you heard anything from Mary or Han lately? I should like to hear. Tell Jeff he must write, and you must, too, mother. I have been in one of the worst hospitals all the forenoon, it containing about 1600. I have given the men pipes and tobacco. (I am the only one that gives them tobacco.) O how much good it does some

The Wound Dresser

of them — the chaplains and most of the doctors are down upon it — but I give them and let them smoke. To others I have given oranges, fed them, etc. Well, dear mother, good-bye — love to Matty and Sis. WALT.

Fred McReady is coming home very soon on furlough — have any of the soldiers called on you?

XXV

Washington, June 3, 1864. DEAREST MOTHER — Your letter came yesterday. I have not heard the least thing from the 51st since — no doubt they are down there with the army near Richmond. I have not written to George lately. I think the news from the Army is very good. Mother, you know of course that it is now very near Richmond indeed, from five to ten miles. Mother, if this campaign was not in progress I should not stop here, as it is now beginning to tell a little upon me, so many bad wounds, many putrefied, and all kinds of dreadful ones, I have been rather too much with — but as it is, I certainly remain here while the thing remains undecided. It is impossible for me to abstain from going to see and minister to certain cases, and that draws me into others, and so on. I have just left Oscar Cunningham, the Ohio boy — he is in a dying condition — there is no hope for him — it would draw tears from the hardest heart to look at him

Letters of 1864

— he is all wasted away to a skeleton, and looks like some one fifty years old. You remember I told you a year ago, when he was first brought in, I thought him the noblest specimen of a young Western man I had seen, a real giant in size, and always with a smile on his face. O what a change. He has long been very irritable to every one but me, and his frame is all wasted away. The young Massachusetts 1st artillery boy, Cutter, I wrote about is dead. He is the one that was brought in a week ago last Sunday badly wounded in breast. The deaths in the principal hospital I visit, Armory-square, average one an hour.

I saw Capt. Baldwin of the 14th this morning; he has lost his left arm — is going home soon. Mr. Kalbfleisch and Anson Herrick, (M. C. from New York) came in one of the wards where I was sitting writing a letter this morning, in the midst of the wounded. Kalbfleisch was so much affected by the sight that he burst into tears. O, I must tell you, I [gave] in Carver hospital a great treat of ice cream, a couple of days ago — went round myself through about 15 large wards — (I bought some ten gallons, very nice). You would have cried and been amused too. Many of the men had to be fed; several of them I saw cannot probably live, yet they quite enjoyed it. I gave everybody some — quite a number [of] Western country boys had never tasted ice cream before. They relish such things [as] oranges, lemons, etc. Mother, I feel a little blue this morning, as two young men I knew very well have just died. One died last

The Wound Dresser

night, and the other about half an hour before I went to the hospital. I did not anticipate the death of either of them. Each was a very, very sad case, so young. Well mother, I see I have written you another gloomy sort of letter. I do not feel as first rate as usual. WALT.

You don't know how I want to come home and see you all; you, dear mother, and Jeff and Mat and all. I believe I am homesick — something new for me — then I have seen all the horrors of soldiers' life and not been kept up by its excitement. It is awful to see so much, and not be able to relieve it.

XXVI

Washington, June 7, 1864. DEAREST MOTHER — I cannot write you anything about the 51st, as I have not heard a word. I felt very much disturbed yesterday afternoon, as Major Hapgood came up from the paymaster general's office, and said that news had arrived that Burnside was killed, and that the 9th Corps had had a terrible slaughter. He said it was believed at the paymaster general's office. Well, I went out to see what reliance there was on it. The rumor soon spread over town, and was believed by many — but as near as I can make it out, it proves to be one of those unaccountable stories that get started these times. Saturday night we heard

Letters of 1864

that Grant was routed completely, etc. etc. — so that's the way stories fly. I suppose you hear the same big lies there in Brooklyn. Well, the truth is sad enough, without adding anything to it — but Grant is not destroyed yet, but I think is going into Richmond yet, but the cost is terrible. Mother, I have not felt well at all the last week. I had spells of deathly faintness and bad trouble in my head too, and sore throat (quite a little budget, ain't they?) My head was the worst, though I don't know, the faint spells were not very pleasant — but I feel so much better this forenoon I believe it has passed over. There is a very horrible collection in Armory building, (in Armory-square hospital) — about 200 of the worst cases you ever see, and I had been probably too much with them. It is enough to melt the heart of a stone; over one third of them are amputation cases. Well, mother, poor Oscar Cunningham is gone at last. He is the 82d Ohio boy (wounded May 3d, '63). I have written so much of him I suppose you feel as if you almost knew him. I was with him Saturday forenoon and also evening. He was more composed than usual, could not articulate very well. He died about 2 o'clock Sunday morning — very easy they told me. I was not there. It was a blessed relief; his life has been misery for months. The cause of death at last was the system absorbing the pus, the bad matter, instead of discharging it from [the] wound. I believe I told you I was quite blue from the deaths of

The Wound Dresser

several of the poor young men I knew well, especially two I had strong hopes of their getting up. Things are going pretty badly with the wounded. They are crowded here in Washington in immense numbers, and all those that come up from the Wilderness and that region, arrived here so neglected, and in such plight, it was awful — (those that were at Fredericksburg and also from Ball Plain). The papers are full of puffs, etc., but the truth is, the largest proportion of worst cases got little or no attention. We receive them here with their wounds full of worms — some all swelled and inflamed. Many of the amputations have to be done over again. One new feature is that many of the poor afflicted young men are crazy. Every ward has some in it that are wandering. They have suffered too much, and it is perhaps a privilege that they are out of their senses. Mother, it is most too much for a fellow, and I sometimes wish I was out of it — but I suppose it is because I have not felt first rate myself. I am going to write to George to-day, as I see there is a daily mail to White House. O, I must tell you that we get the wounded from our present field near Richmond much better than we did from the Wilderness and Fredericksburg. We get them now from White House. They are put on boats there, and come all the way here, about 160 or 170 miles. White House is only twelve or fifteen miles from the field, and is our present depot and base of supplies. It is very pleasant

Letters of 1864

here to-day, a little cooler than it has been — a good rain shower last evening. The Western reg'ts continue to pour in here, the 100 days men; — may go down to front to guard posts, trains, etc.

Well, mother, how do things go on with you all? It seems to me if I could only be home two or three days, and have some good teas with you and Mat, and set in the old basement a while, and have a good time and talk with Jeff, and see the little girls, etc., I should be willing to keep on afterward among these sad scenes for the rest of the summer — but I shall remain here until this Richmond campaign is settled, anyhow, unless I get sick, and I don't anticipate that. Mother dear, I hope you are well and in fair spirits — you must try to. Have you heard from sister Han? WALT.

You know I am living at 502 Pennsylvania av. (near 3d st.) — it is not a very good place. I don't like it so well as I did cooking my own grub — and the air is not good. Jeff, you must write.

XXVII

Washington, June 10, 1864. DEAREST MOTHER — I got your letter dated last Wednesday. I do not always depend on ———'s accounts. I think he is apt to make things full as bad as they are, if not worse.

The Wound Dresser

Mother, I was so glad to get a letter from Jeff this morning, enclosing one from George dated June 1st. It was so good to see his handwriting once more. I have not heard anything of the reg't — there are all sorts of rumors here, among others that Burnside does not give satisfaction to Grant and Meade, and that it is expected some one else will be placed in command of 9th Corps. Another rumor more likely is that our base of the army is to be changed to Harrison's Landing on James river instead of White House on Pamunkey.

Mother, I have not felt well again the last two days as I was Tuesday, but I feel a good deal better this morning. I go round, but most of the time feel very little like it. The doctor tells me I have continued too long in the hospitals, especially in a bad place, Armory building, where the worst wounds were, and have absorbed too much of the virus in my system — but I know it is nothing but what a little relief and sustenance of [the] right sort will set right. I am writing this in Major Hapgood's office. He is very busy paying off some men whose time is out; they are going home to New York. I wrote to George yesterday. We are having very pleasant weather here just now. Mother, you didn't mention whether Mary had come, so I suppose she has not. I should like to see her and Ansel too. The wounded still come here in large numbers — day and night trains of ambulances. Tell Jeff the $10 from Mr. Lane for the soldiers came safe. I shall

Letters of 1864

write to Jeff right away. I send my love to Mat and all. Mother, you must try to keep good heart. WALT.

XXVIII

Washington, June 14, 1864. DEAREST MOTHER. I am not feeling very well these days — the doctors have told me not to come inside the hospitals for the present. I send there by a friend every day; I send things and aid to some cases I know, and hear from there also, but I do not go myself at present. It is probable that the hospital poison has affected my system, and I find it worse than I calculated. I have spells of faintness and very bad feeling in my head, fullness and pain — and besides sore throat. My boarding place, 502 Pennsylvania av., is a miserable place, very bad air. But I shall feel better soon, I know — the doctors say it will pass over — they have long told me I was going in too strong. Some days I think it has all gone and I feel well again, but in a few hours I have a spell again. Mother, I have not heard anything of the 51st. I sent George's letter to Han. I have written to George since. I shall write again to him in a day or two. If Mary comes home, tell her I sent her my love. If I don't feel better before the end of this week or beginning of next, I may come home for a week or

The Wound Dresser

fortnight for a change. The rumor is very strong here that Grant is over the James river on south side — but it is not in the papers. We are having quite cool weather here. Mother, I want to see you and Jeff so much. I have been working a little at copying, but have stopt it lately. WALT.

XXIX

Washington, June 17, 1864. DEAREST MOTHER. I got your letter this morning. This place and the hospitals seem to have got the better of me. I do not feel so badly this forenoon — but I have bad nights and bad days too. Some of the spells are pretty bad — still I am up some and around every day. The doctors have told me for a fortnight I must leave; that I need an entire change of air, etc.

I think I shall come home for a short time, and pretty soon. (I will try it two or three days yet though, and if I find my illness goes over I will stay here yet awhile. All I think about is to be here if any thing should happen to George).

We don't hear anything more of the army than you do there in the papers. WALT.

Mother, if I should come I will write a day or so before.

Letters of 1864

The letter of June 17, 1864, is the last of Whitman's, written from Washington at or about this time, that has been preserved and come down to us. Many, probably many more than have been kept, have been lost; indeed, it is a wonder that so many were saved, for they were sent about from one member of the family to another, and when once read seem to have been little valued. The reader will have noticed a certain change of tone in the later letters, showing that Whitman was beginning to feel the inroads which the fatigues, the unhealthy surroundings of the hospitals, and especially the mental anxiety and distress inseparable from his work there, were making upon even his superb health. Down to the time of his hospital work he had never known a day's sickness, but thereafter he never again knew, except at intervals which grew shorter and less frequent as time went on, the buoyant vigor and vitality of his first forty-four years. From 1864 to the end of 1872 the attacks described in his "Calamus" letters became from year to year more frequent and more severe, until, in January, 1873, they culminated in an attack of paralysis which never left him and from the indirect effects of which he died in 1892.

But for years, though often warned and sent away by the doctors, during his better intervals and until his splendid health was quite broken by hospital malaria and the poison absorbed from gangrenous wounds, he continued his ministrations to the sick and the maimed of the war. Those who joined the ranks and fought the battles of the Republic did

The Wound Dresser

well; but when the world knows, as it is beginning to know, how this man, without any encouragement from without, under no compulsion, simply, without beat of drum or any cheers of approval, went down into those immense lazar houses and devoted his days and nights, his heart and soul, and at last his health and life, to America's sick and wounded sons, it will say that he did even better.

R. M. B.

As at thy portals also death,
Entering thy sovereign, dim, illimitable grounds,
To memories of my mother, to the divine blending, maternity,
To her, buried and gone, yet buried not, gone not from me,
(I see again the calm benignant face fresh and beautiful still,
I sit by the form in the coffin,
I kiss and kiss convulsively again the sweet old lips, the cheeks, the closed eyes in the coffin;)
To her, the ideal woman, practical, spiritual, of all of earth, life, love, to me the best,
I grave a monumental line, before I go, amid these songs,
And set a tombstone here.

www.ingramcontent.com/pod-product-compliance
Lightning Source LLC
Chambersburg PA
CBHW031819220426
43662CB00007B/713